ENTREPRENEURSHIP STARTER GUIDE FOR BEGINNERS AND PROFESSIONALS 2023

INDEPENDENT ENTREPRENEUR

By

KYLIE GREENER

DISCLAIMER

This book is dedicated to Penny's Brothers, Aaron Strong - great leaders build confidence and esteem in their people, while simultaneously inspiring them and challenging them to raise the bar and perform at their very best. Your ability to demonstrate this leadership skills was invaluable to us when writing this book, so thank you.

To new entrepreneurs.
To those who work yet struggle.
To those who struggle to work.
To those who invent, or write, or dream without financing.
To those inventors or entrepreneurs without funding.

You are the unsung heroes of innovation- the discontented geniuses too often left without witness.

Find here tools to thrive in a world which prevents you from achieving your potential yet punishes lack of success.

AUTHORS NOTE

This book contains frequently used
research and methods. Where we know
the source we have been sure to
reference it, but our apologies here to
the originators of any material if we
have overlooked them

ABOUT THE AUTHOR

Kylie Greener is an economic consultant specializing in job research and financial strategy. Besides authoring a variety of books on economics, finance, and strategy. She has taught graduate-level courses at a variety of Universities in the US. and China and is currently involved in the MBA Programme at Bellevue University in the US. She has assisted major organizations from around the world in their development for strategic resource management, including the U.S. Department of Defense, the American Red Cross, Ocean Audit, Inc. in the Czech Republic and Saving Humanity in Australia.

ABOUT THIS BOOK

ENTREPRENEUR

An entrepreneur is someone who starts and runs businesses. They could be an inventor: someone who has created a new product or service. It is a job that requires creativity, patience, excellent communication skills, and self-assurance.

They want freedom and power.
As an entrepreneur, you want to be your own boss while also having complete control over all aspects of your company. This preference is frequently the reason why traditional jobs aren't a good fit for entrepreneurs, as they

provide neither and may not feel like a challenge.

TABLE OF CONTENTS

PART 1

WHY SHOULD YOU BECOME AN ENTREPRENEUR

There are numerous reasons to consider entrepreneurship, ranging from its freedom and flexibility to the job satisfaction it can provide.

Be your own boss.
This is the career for you if you like to be in charge. You will make all major business decisions. You may have colleagues and advisors, but ultimately, the operation of the business is your responsibility. It's an opportunity to

demonstrate excellent leadership while also getting the most out of others.

Potentially unlimited income

Unlike working for a company, where your salary is determined by someone else, when you own your own business, your income is determined solely by you. You can reward yourself if you work hard and the business is successful. Being an entrepreneur is high risk, high reward - you could make millions or nothing at all. However, the earning potential is greater than in almost any other occupation.

Work when and where you want.

Being an entrepreneur is one of the most adaptable jobs available. You make your own schedule, deciding when to work hard and when to take a break. It's a true blessing to be able to work around your schedule rather than the other way around.

Earn a living doing what you enjoy. Start-ups are among the most exciting and fast-paced workplaces. You will not be bored because things are constantly changing. You will enjoy the challenge of competing with other businesses to provide your customers with the best service or product. You might also be able to build a successful business out of something you truly care about.

Constant growth and development
Being your own boss is not easy, nor is running a business. You must be brave,

take risks, and believe in yourself. You must also be able to solve problems and admit when something has gone wrong. Staying positive, thinking creatively, and being solution-minded are all valuable skills that will serve you well in life and business.

Choose who you want to collaborate with.

When you run your own business, you form your own team. You can surround yourself with people who share your vision and work the way you want them to. One of the most rewarding aspects of being a manager is being able to develop new talent and get the most out of your coworkers.

Make a positive difference.
Starting and running a business allows you to make a positive difference. Whether it's uplifting society, creating jobs in your community, or leading the way in sustainable business and demonstrating how to protect the environment.

satisfying and rewarding
Building your own successful business is a significant accomplishment. It will always have challenges, but when things go well, it is even more rewarding. You will be able to look back on your accomplishments and know that they were the result of your own hard work.

What is the definition of social entrepreneurship?

Social entrepreneurship is the creation and funding of ventures that address larger social issues. Social entrepreneurs want to use their business skills and knowledge to make a bigger difference in the world, from local communities to society as a whole. People frequently mix up social entrepreneurship and nonprofit organizations such as charities. It is important to note that social entrepreneurship is still primarily concerned with making a profit, but there is a greater emphasis on making changes that benefit people first. What you choose to focus on, from environmental to societal, will be determined by your personal interests or a need identified through thorough research.

What is the significance of entrepreneurship?

Entrepreneurs start new businesses, which contribute to national income through taxation. New businesses generate fresh, innovative ideas for products that can benefit people in their daily lives.

As a social entrepreneur, your company will have a direct and positive impact on society.

What is the role of entrepreneurship in the economy?

All businesses begin with an idea, and those ideas can grow and develop into full-fledged businesses that profit and have a significant impact on the world. Developing new products and services generates new job opportunities and boosts economic growth.

PART 2

EMOTIONAL ROLLERCOASTER IN BUSINESS

Entrepreneurs may experience an emotional rollercoaster, with peaks and valleys alternating between high pressure, stress, and uncertainty, and relative calm and early accomplishments. This may cause emotional strain for entrepreneurs who must deal with these abrupt shifts between success and disappointment.

In life, you have to make a lot of decisions. So, if you want to be a successful entrepreneur, you must be aware that when you are an entrepreneur, your emotions (e.g. happiness, sadness) are multiplied when compared to when you are employed. This is referred to as the emotional rollercoaster of being an entrepreneur.

Building a business can make you feel insane. You must have been there, right?

Riding the rollercoaster
Simply put, there are only two emotions: joy and pain. These emotions either create a high or a low state in us. Our suffering results from our constant striving for the high and avoiding the low. And this is where the roller coaster

begins to race up and down between highs and lows.

If we are unconscious, we live from victory to victory, exaggerate the smallest setbacks, and no longer appreciate the process in between.

Small victories validate us, but when they don't happen, we become insecure. When minor setbacks occur, we become discouraged and ready to give up. Perhaps you did not receive the desired feedback, your offer did not sell, or clients dumped you.
At the same time, when we get a new client, win an important pitch, or have 10,000 views on our Instagram reel, we feel invincible. On top of the world.

We believe that our future is determined by our successes and failures.

We overestimate both our losses and our victories. Tremendously.
However, both of these situations, the win and the setback, are just snapshots of reality. They do not represent the entirety of the film.
This overestimation of circumstances causes an emotional roller coaster. The only way out is to get off the rollercoaster.
But how exactly? Great question, and I'm glad you asked.

You are not your Emotions.
Emotions fluctuate depending on the situation.
They never appear in a vacuum, but only when we are confronted with our surroundings, other people, or even just ourselves.
The emotion would not exist if the current situation did not exist. As a result, you must be aware that you are not your emotions.
You are not angry if you are enraged by an argument, but you feel angry. At that point, the anger has taken possession of you, and you can choose to distance yourself from it again.

Life and business come in waves; if we can accept that, we will find peace. Apart from external circumstances such as successes or setbacks, many natural forces affect and influence our emotions.

Depending on where we are in our monthly cycle, we can handle certain setbacks better or worse. We have more energy during the waxing moon than during the waning moon. We can deal with problems better during the day than at night.

So hormones, cycles, natural phenomena, and insignificant details all have an impact on us. Because everything is constantly in motion, it feels like a roller coaster ride of emotions.

The first steps to getting off the roller coaster are to recognize that you are not your emotions and that life is cyclical and thus never the same.

The following step is to change your emotions.

Put yourself in a State of Constant Gratitude.

Gratitude does not happen to you. You made it happen.

Gratitude is a conscious decision to be appreciative, respectful, and thankful. Whatever the case may be.

We do not distinguish between good and bad in a Constant State of Gratitude. We don't pass judgment, but rather accept the situation as it is and make the best of it.

You observe feelings without becoming emotionally involved with them. What you're going through is a critical situation for you to grow. You are always at ease.

From: What is happening to me?
To: How can I benefit from it?

Have you landed a major project? Excellent; be grateful for the opportunity to learn. Did your customer abandon you? Excellent; be grateful for the opportunity to learn.

Our emotions are balanced by gratitude. This equilibrium allows us to stay on track, keep our heads clear, and achieve our goals.

Every time we feel like we're on an emotional roller coaster, it's a sign that we've lost our equilibrium. We have the impression that we are losing sight of our objective or vision.

In a Constant State of Gratitude, you see situations as necessary lessons and don't let your emotions cause you to fall into a high or low.

But that doesn't mean you have to be able to handle every situation. Be grateful for the learning experience, and then decide whether to leave it, love it, or change it.

Can I influence the situation? Can I accept the situation joyfully, or can I recognize it as a lesson and accept it as it is?

In either case, you can be grateful for the situation and stop putting so much

emphasis on the minor wins and losses that come and go.
That doesn't mean you can't be happy or angry, but don't place too much emphasis on it.

Extreme emotions deviate us from our goals. Emotions will always be present in our lives, but how much we let them guide us is entirely up to us.
Consider the big picture and have faith that the situation is critical for a higher purpose.

Life and business comes in waves; it's more fun if we learn how to surf.
Sometimes you have 20 customers or projects at once and you don't know

what to do, and other times you don't have a single one.

Believe that this is exactly what you require right now. Perhaps there are no clients, allowing you to focus on your new website or another project you've been putting off for a long time. Gratitude gives me the peace and serenity I need to deal with difficult situations while staying on track.

Sure, emotions will still surface, but the roller coaster you can't get off becomes more like a short whirlwind.

How to Improve Your Gratitude

Gratitude journaling is extremely popular right now. Nonetheless, I believe that many people automate the ritual of writing down three things for which they are grateful. But this is not sustainable in the long run.

Gratitude has an impact only when it is genuine.

It's not what you write that matters; it's how you feel. So close your eyes and immerse yourself in thankfulness.

What exactly is happening right now? Where do you see potential for learning? What are you grateful for?

Remember that life is always in motion. Both the good and the bad will pass. There's no need to overestimate these emotions; instead, let them serve as a teacher. You're going to be fine. You've got this.

You are a human being. You have feelings, emotions, and beliefs. What you do next is influenced by how you feel at the time. When you are in a good mood, you are more likely to concentrate on what will help your business grow and conquer your to-do list. When you don't feel well, your brain and body tell you to avoid tasks and binge-watch your favorite Netflix series.

Having control over your emotions is a superpower. It's the difference between productive and wasteful days. Elite business owners understand this. They consistently work on personal development to better understand themselves. Self-awareness allows them to ride the emotional roller coaster without vomiting. Building a profitable business necessitates focusing on these three factors.

Learn how to perform at your best.
When your feelings and emotions start to spiral, the power and importance of getting back into peak state. The idea is that once something triggers you, you should acknowledge everything you're feeling. Process your feelings and emotions so they don't fester and take root in your mind.

You then alter your state. This can occur through physical movement, music, or conversation. Whatever is convenient for you. But you return to a strong mental state that allows you to maintain control. All of this occurs in less than a minute. The more you do this exercise, the better you will become at getting back to your strongest self.

Learning how to regain peak performance is a game changer. It enables you to regain control of your feelings and emotions. Consider peak-performance athletes and what they accomplish in their sport. The same holds true for us as business owners.

Determine your overall life strategy. The first step in getting somewhere is knowing where you're going. Many entrepreneurs get caught up in the tactics. They rush from task to task, oblivious to the fact that their actions have no significant impact on the big picture.

Doing entrepreneurial tasks makes sense only if they are aligned with your overall business strategy. You must understand who your company serves and what problems it solves. A clear vision, mission statement, and operational guidelines are required. You must comprehend your brand's strategy. What tasks you work on each day should be dictated by those main strategy components. Imposter syndrome and self-limiting beliefs can be combated by being clear about your strategy. Clarity is a source of great power. Don't get caught up in the hustle and bustle of your job.

Improve and train your mind.

Because your brain is a muscle that can be trained, optimize it by putting in the effort every day. Feed your mind with content that challenges your preconceived notions and forces you to think.

Don't reach for your phone and begin filling your mind with life's distractions the moment you wake up. Instead, provide it with motivational content in the form of videos, audio, or books. Use the time you wake up to meditate and center yourself.

Begin your day by exercising your mind. It's the first step toward winning the day's emotional battles because your mind will be in a stronger state. Make time in your life and business to work on mind-training exercises. You can hire coaches, take courses, learn how the brain works, and do a variety of other things.

Gaining control is your secret weapon for experiencing explosive growth in your business this year. Don't let your feelings and emotions make decisions for you. It's a bad place to be. Take back your power by doing the work on a daily basis.

WHY DOES THE EMOTIONAL ROLLERCOASTER EXIST?

I believe that a high risk of outcome results in increased variance of emotions (e.g. secure outcome, keeping cool or high potential payoff, super enthusiastic when things are going well), which is the root cause of the emotional rollercoaster.

As an entrepreneur, your company will either be successful or not (e.g. measured by the appreciation in equity value). When you test your product-market fit (talking to potential clients, working on a website feature, talking to investors), your expectations will change because you automatically extrapolate the test data into the future. This is the beginning of the emotional rollercoaster! Superstars may face a similar situation.

BEING ON THE EMOTIONAL ROLLERCOASTER!

Let me walk you through two scenarios that you might encounter on your entrepreneurial journey.

1. FROM HEAVEN TO HELL - You are in this situation when you receive bad news and extrapolate it into the future, leading you to believe that all is lost (aka forget about that equity portion you hold:-)).

Consider the following examples.

* **Losing an important client**; imagine your major client, who is responsible for 30% of your sales, calling you at 5 p.m. to tell you that he will now buy from your competitor. What do you

think? How do you feel? I'll tell you what I think. "This [please insert a really, really bad word] wants to destroy my business. Who does he think he is? God? I have 30 employees who rely on me and my company. Arrrr!" Have you been in a similar situation? Welcome to the emotional rollercoaster that is being an entrepreneur!

* **Investor meeting gone wrong** - your company is expanding, and you are pleased with yourself. What a lovely world we live in. Now all you need is a cash infusion because your operating cash flow is refusing to turn positive. As a result, you're in discussions with some well-known investors about selling a portion of your equity in exchange for cash. The initial meetings went extremely well, and you now have

two potential investors. "Dear [enter your first name here], as you may have read in the newspapers, we acquired an equity stake in your competitor," says the first potential investor in your inbox. As a result, we will not proceed with your investment proposal." The good news is that you have one more potential investor. So you enter the final negotiations cheerfully.

* **During the meeting**, the investor inquires about your operational performance and discovers a deal breaker that he was not previously aware of. Damn! We lost our last potential investor, and we don't have enough time before our cash runs out to raise capital. Arrrr!

* **2. FROM HELL TO HEAVEN** - This is a situation in which you receive

good news and extrapolate it into the future, leading you to believe that you are the next Mark Zuckerberg or Bill Gates. Let me show you what I mean.

* **Performance indicators significantly above plan** - You are 12 months into your next startup and discover that your customer acquisition costs, conversion rates, sales, and profit margins are significantly higher than expected. What do you think? How do you feel? If you are skeptical, you may believe that you have miscalculated your KPIs. Fortunately, your calculations were correct. You can already see yourself as the next mega-entrepreneur adored by newspapers, girls, and banks (for the money). You throw a party for your employees and appear to be living in a dream.

SURVIVING THE ROLLERCOASTER

You are now familiar with the emotional rollercoaster that is in entrepreneurship. If these situations are unavoidable (from heaven to hell, from hell to heaven), what can you do to prepare so that you can focus on growing your business?

SIMPLE FORMULA: manage your expectations while focusing more on doing be less swayed by a rollercoaster

Let's go over each of these drivers in depth so you know exactly what to do.

1. MANAGING YOUR EXPECTATIONS -

When you're riding the emotional rollercoaster that is entrepreneurship, you need to manage your expectations through a process I call rationalization. When you are down, rationalization helps you improve your emotions; when you are overjoyed, rationalization helps you put your emotions into perspective. Let me illustrate my point with two examples.

* If you are depressed and angry because you have lost a very important client, visualize your company going out of business and what you will do then (aka your second best alternative).

Then, on a scale of 1 to 10, rate the second best alternative (Unbearable to Awesome). I am confident that after giving the second best alternative some thought, you will not rate it less than 5 stars, because you know you learned a lot during your entrepreneurial journey, made some valuable contacts, and can restart with a new, possibly even better business idea.

* If you are overjoyed because you signed a double-digit investment round with well-known investors, take a step back and ask yourself what this means for your business. Without a doubt, receiving funding is fantastic. However, the difficult part is only beginning - growing your business. Do you think businesses that receive bank funding

(aka debt funding) celebrate as much as entrepreneurs who receive equity funding? You must be certain that this emotionally uplifting situation will be successful. As a result, any distraction from your business should be avoided as much as possible.

2. FOCUS ON DOING - As an entrepreneur, you must balance the visionary (aka long-term planning) and operational parts of your business (aka doing the stuff that improves your business). If the emotional rollercoaster begins, you are too focused on the long term future while ignoring the short term aspects of running the business. As a result, if you are experiencing an emotional rollercoaster, stay focused on sales, operations, and improving your

KPIs. Your company and investors will appreciate it.

As a result of managing your expectations and focusing on doing, you will be less sensitive to the emotional rollercoaster and thus more productive because you will not be as easily distracted from what is important - growing your business.

PART 3

IDENTIFYING YOUR NICHE

For entrepreneurs, there are two options. You can either serve the general public or a specific niche market. Entrepreneurs who serve a large market typically create a wide range of products or work in multiple industries. They are, however, struggling to become the market leader in each of their offerings.

Knowing your ideal clients within your specific niche is the most important aspect of starting and running a successful business.

Your target audience is a group of people who share similar demographics, interests, values, and beliefs. It will be much easier to identify your target audience if you are clear about your specific niche. Once you've determined who your target audience is, you'll be able to implement your marketing strategy, including the content and product development processes. As a result, selecting a niche should never be underestimated.

Determine your interests and skills. The best way to choose a niche is to first decide what you enjoy and are good at. You will be able to monetize your passion and skill in this manner. With the two key factors combined, you will be able to lay a solid foundation for your business. Doing something you are passionate about will keep you motivated in the long run because you are doing something you enjoy. This will be your main motivation when you feel like giving up. If you are doing something you dislike, you are more likely to quit because it is more difficult to stay motivated.

When you choose something you enjoy, you will naturally excel at it. When you are good at what you enjoy doing, you will be able to solve problems in that market because you are utilizing a skill set that you already possess.

Determine your target audience's issues.

Building a profitable business requires understanding your target audience's problems and desires and being able to bridge the gap to help them get to where they want to go. To solve their problems, you must first understand what they are dealing with.

So how do you know what kinds of issues they're dealing with? We can easily search for keywords on Google to find out what pain points our potential customers are experiencing because we have the internet at our fingertips. Facebook groups and Quora are great places to find out what questions people are asking. They are also excellent locations for market research. Examine the discussions going on and try to notice what questions people are asking and what problems they are having.

Investigate your competition. It is critical to understand your competition in order to determine market profitability. Understanding your competitors will allow you to identify market gaps and fill them. You'll get to develop your own unique value proposition and determine whether the market is oversaturated or not. Knowing your competitors will give you an idea of how to outrank them by studying their strengths and weaknesses. Competitor analysis and performance monitoring will help you be well-prepared to make improvements along the way.

Determine your potential profit. As you gather information for your market research, you should have an idea of the profitability of your niche. Choosing an evergreen industry is one way to ensure that your company will be profitable in the long run. Some markets outperform others because they are evergreen, meaning there is always demand in those markets. Google Trends can be used to conduct market research by identifying trending topics and keywords that are frequently searched. It is critical to ascertain whether the niche you have selected is in demand and whether people are willing to pay for what you have to offer.

Validate your Idea

The last thing you want to do before deciding on a niche is validate your idea by running a test. You can validate your product idea and raise funds by using crowdfunding websites like Kickstarter. You can also create a landing page on MailChimp and begin collecting leads to see how well the promotion goes and whether the niche you choose has any demand. One quick way to do this is to run a few paid ads to direct users to your landing page and track the performance of your ads.

The worst thing that can happen is that you choose a low-demand niche, register your company, and have your website up and running only to discover that no one wants your products or services. These are mistakes you can avoid if you follow all of the steps above before finalizing your niche and getting things up and running.

Create a solid foundation

Conducting market research and competitor analysis may appear exhausting, but every startup must lay a solid foundation. It is critical to understand your competitors as well as your customers in order to constantly improve your marketing. When you do this, you are gradually strengthening your unique value proposition and building a distinct brand.

This is not the case for entrepreneurs in a niche market. These business owners create specific products or serve specific audiences. Serving a niche market helps you gain credibility and become the go-to brand for your audience, in addition to narrowing your scope.

In this Guide, you'll learn about the benefits of niche markets, how to find your niche, and what to do once you've identified an unmet need.

What is the definition of a niche market?

Advantages of a Niche Market

How to Find a Niche Market

Example of a Niche Market

Find Your Place in a Niche Market

What is the definition of a niche market?

A niche market is a specific group of people or businesses who want to buy a particular product or service. Consider niche marketing to be the act of specializing in what you provide.

When your company offers specific products and services rather than a wide range of options, you save money and become more productive. You will also gain a competitive advantage over generalist competitors.

Animals such as dogs and cats, for example, are used in the pet industry. Creating a business that sells dog collars is a niche market. The same is true for cat sweaters and pet GPS trackers.

When a company chooses to sell to a specific market, it attracts more customers to their product or service. Let's take a look at some of the advantages of operating in a niche market.

The Advantages of a Niche Market

Niche marketing is an effective way to establish your brand positioning whether you're starting or scaling a business. Here are some additional advantages that niche market entrepreneurs enjoy.

Effective Marketing Resource Utilization

You can use your resources to find customers who are interested in your product if you focus on a small audience. These are the people who require your product the most and are most likely to convert.

Niche marketing can also help you save money on marketing and advertising. This is because a highly targeted audience necessitates fewer buyer personas. You can spend wisely by focusing on specific types of prospects.

More Social Evidence

Aligning your products or services with a small group of customers is an excellent way to encourage positive word-of-mouth marketing and reviews. This type of social proof is extremely powerful. Recommendations can help your company enter a larger and potentially more profitable market. Niche markets frequently evolve into mass markets. So, while you're starting small today, think about the big picture and start laying the groundwork for long-term success.

Less Competition

Working in a niche market means you'll face little to no competition. Many businesses or individuals prefer to serve a large number of customers. By being specific, you will eliminate many companies from your customers' radar. However, there may be fewer customers looking for your product or service. As a result, you'll need to enter a niche market with a large enough audience.

Enhanced Brand Loyalty

Individuals and businesses can increase brand loyalty through niche marketing. Engaging with fewer people allows you to nurture prospects and build quality relationships more easily. Your audience will sense that you are tuned in to their energy. They will see you as a true partner, not a vendor who is only interested in their money.

How to Locate a Niche Market

* Consider your passions and interests.
* Determine your customers' problems and needs.
* Do your homework on the competition.
* Determine your niche's profitability.
* Put your product or service to the test.

1. Consider your interests and passions.

Is there a hobby or skill you enjoy or excel at? Consider those areas of interest as potential niche market ideas. Here are some questions to get you started:

* What abilities do I have?
* How do I approach problem solving?
* What subjects do I enjoy learning about?
* How do I spend my free time?
* Do my friends, family, and coworkers ask me for advice on a specific topic?

Writing your responses to these questions will assist you in identifying your core strengths. This allows you to expand on a niche market idea that you already enjoy.

2. Determine your customers' problems and requirements.

Now that you have some niche market ideas, consider the problems that your target market faces. Can your passion or interest meet your customers' needs? Do you know why they bought?
Conducting market research will assist you in determining customer purchasing habits and challenges.

There are numerous tools (some of which are free) for researching your customer persona. Using them gives you a better idea of how your company can add value to your niche market.

3. Research the competition

Investigate your potential competitors before devoting your time and energy to developing a brand-new business. You may have a viable product idea, but how many other businesses will you be competing with?

This is where research tools come in handy. Let us look at a few of them.

Topics for Exploration

Exploding Topics is an excellent tool for entrepreneurs to identify emerging trends before they take off. This is how it works.

Assume you're interested in the beauty niche. To find emerging trends, go to explodingtopics.com and use the "All categories" filter. When you click "Beauty," you'll get something like this.

Beauty Trends

The hottest beauty topics, brands, products and industry trends.

SORT BY: Past 5 Years | Beauty | G Search Database

Aklief	6.6K	+1975%
Somethinc	110	+7100%
Bakuchiol	14.8K	+9700%

Brand that's best known for creating bifarotene, a medicated acne treatment cream.

Halal-certified skincare and makeup brand.

Medicinal plant extract that can be used for skin care to reduce dark circles and smooth fine lines.

You can then see your competitors in that market and figure out how to stand out.

Google Trends

Let's say "Bakuchiol" from the beauty trends piques your interest. A competitive research tool like Google Trends can tell you how frequently people search for this term.

As shown in the graph below, interest in the term has been steadily increasing in the United States since 2017.

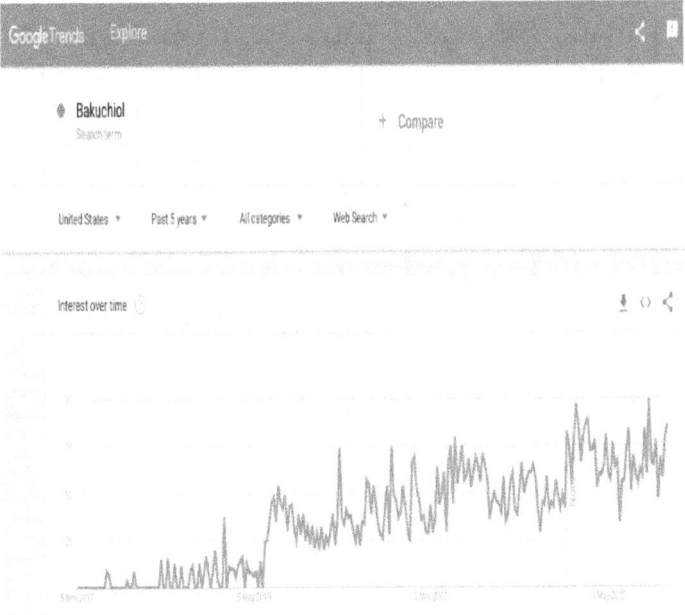

This information can be used to estimate market size and demand.

Respond to the Public

Use a tool like Answer The Public to find a niche for different product categories to find a market around your search term.

For example, if we search Answer The Public for "Bakuchiol for," we'll get 331 results, including bakuchiol for acne, body, blackheads, breastfeeding, skincare, and face.

205 Alphabeticals: bakuchiol for

a — View Image

bakuchiol for acne
bakuchiol for acne scars
bakuchiol for anti aging
bakuchiol for acne prone skin
bakuchiol for acne reddit
bakuchiol for age spots
bakuchiol with aha bha
bakuchiol with azelaic acid

b — View Image

bakuchiol for body
bakuchiol for blackheads
bakuchiol for breastfeeding
bakuchiol for beginners
bakuchiol benefits for skin
bakuchiol safe for breastfeeding
bakuchiol benefits
bakuchiol before and after

c — View Image

bakuchiol for cystic acne
bakuchiol for skin care
bakuchiol for dark circles
bakuchiol canada
bakuchiol + cbd
bakuchiol cena
bakuchiol complete cosmedix
bakuchio comedogenic rating

d — View Image

bakuchiol for dry skin
bakuchiol for dark spots
bakuchiol for dark circles
bakuchiol during pregnancy
bakuchiol day cream
bakuchiol dr dray
bakuchiol definition
bakuchiol do not mix

e — View Image

bakuchiol for eyes
bakuchiol for eczema
bakuchiol for eye wrinkles
bakuchiol serum for eyes
bakuchiol bad for environment
bakuchiol eye cream
bakuchiol extract
bakuchiol ewg

f — View Image

bakuchiol for face
bakuchiol for fine lines
bakuchiol oil for face
bakuchiol flower
bakuchiol female daily
bakuchiol function
bakuchiol face mask
bakuchiol fungal acne

Each result offers a niche opportunity for you to investigate.

Ubersuggest

However, before committing to any keyword, use a free keyword research tool like Ubersuggest to get a detailed overview of each term.

For example, when we enter "bakuchiol for acne," we see that it has a high-paid difficulty and a low cost per click.

Other tools for competitor research include:
* Google Keyword Planner
* ClickBank
* Amazon

Use these tools to research the best-selling products that consumers are looking for and determine whether your new business can meet their needs.

4. Determine your niche's profitability.

If you're committing your resources and time to a new venture, it should be able to become profitable. Here are a few things to think about when deciding on a niche:

* **The standard of the product**. Is your product handmade, eco-friendly, or of high quality?

* **Price**. Do you want to sell high-end items or will you price them reasonably?

* **The location of the customer**. Where is your intended audience located? Are they located in a specific country or region?

* Customer preferences and interests. Are you looking for vegans, environmentalists, travelers, or sports fans?

* Demographics of customers. Are you selling to straight people or the LGTBQ+ community? What are their ages, education levels, and income levels?

If you research the market and find similar products, your idea could be profitable, but few companies sell them. Examine the price points of competitors' products in order to price yours competitively.

G2 (for software), Amazon (for products) agency directories (for services), and PRICEFY.IO (for price monitoring) are all excellent resources for assessing competitor pricing and determining prices for your own products and services.

5. Put your product or service through testing.

Make a basic website or landing page for your company so that customers can find you. Provide a product trial period or free samples to your target customers. This initial test period should not be expensive. You can, however, use paid advertising to drive traffic to your website.

Use crowdfunding sites to see if people want to contribute to your product. Not only will you be able to raise funds, but you will also be able to get your product in front of potential customers.

Don't abandon your idea if the test isn't as successful as you hoped. Return to the drawing board to identify key areas where your product or marketing can be improved.

If you're wondering what a niche business looks like, here are seven examples of niche businesses.

Examples of Niche Markets
* Georgetown Cupcake
* The Container Store
* Drybar
* SoulCycle
* T*es.com
* Dorm M*m

* Kirrin F*nch

1. Georgetown Cupcake: A bakery that only specializes in cupcakes.

Sisters Katherine Kallinis Berman and Sophie Kallinis LaMontagne pursued their passion for baking after leaving corporate jobs and opened Georgetown Cupcake. Unlike other bakeries that create cakes and other sweets, their sole product is cupcakes, and by focusing on one product type, they were able to perfect their recipes.

2. The Container Store: A store that sells only containers.

Instead of selling furniture, textiles, and artwork, The Container Store focuses on selling compartments — large and small enclosed storage containers where customers put their belongings. Customers could go to a convenience store to buy storage, but there's a good chance they won't find the exact container that fits their cupboard's space and aesthetic.

The Container Store fills that void (literally), and the company has made a good profit in this market.

3. Drybar: A blowout salon that does not provide haircuts or color.

In 2022, the Hair Salon industry in the United States was valued at $48.3 billion. There are certainly enough opportunities for entrepreneurs who want to provide specific services in this industry. As a result, Drybar only provides blow-dry and styling services. The salon offers a few hair-styling options to give customers some variety. What distinguishes Drybar is its distinct concept of focusing on one thing and excelling at it: blowouts.

4. SoulCycle: A fitness center that only offers indoor cycling classes.

SoulCycle is a 45-minute indoor cycling class that distinguishes itself from competitors by only offering one specialized spin class. Other fitness studios pale in comparison to the community of dedicated cyclists who spend hours working out at SoulCycle.

5. Ties.com: A clothing store specializing in men's accessories.

In 2022, global revenue in the men's apparel market was $499.80 billion. The United States alone possessed $100.5 billion. This sum demonstrates the enormous potential of the menswear market, allowing Ties.com to create a niche market that sells specific products.

Ties.com stands out in the menswear market by only selling accessories such as ties, socks, pocket squares, and wallets. Because their products make up a small portion of the menswear industry, they stand out from the competition because they can focus on creating unique, high-quality accessories.

6. Dorm Mom: College students' laundry service.

According to Grand View Research, the global dry-cleaning and laundry services market could be worth $79.91 billion by 2027. People can easily carve out a niche in this industry by offering laundry services to children, men, women, LGBTQ communities, students, and the list goes on.

Dorm Moms took this approach by focusing on a specific audience. Dorm Mom only serves college students rather than a large population of people in need of laundry service.

7. Kirrin Finch: A clothing line for LGBTQ+ people.

In the United States alone, the LGBTQ community has a spending power of approximately $1 trillion. This is an excellent market for brands that support this community. When LGBTQ founders lead the brand, the bond is

even stronger. This is the case with
Kirrin Finch, an LGBTQ clothing line.
Kirrin Finch, led by Kelly and Laura
Moffat, provides bespoke suits and
button-up shirts to members of the
LGBTQ community for weddings,
workwear, or simply to look your best
at all times.

Find Your Place in a Niche Market
Specializing your products and services
in a specific market allows you to better
utilize your resources, produce products
faster, and develop a loyal customer
base. Selling to a niche market can be a
short-term or long-term strategy; the

key is to find your audience and tailor everything you do specifically for them.

PART 4

MARKET RESEARCH AND TESTING

Market testing is a method of testing that market researchers are all too familiar with. Market testing is the holy grail of data, and it generally paves the way for the critical objectives for other types of testing as well.

What precisely is market testing?

Market testing is defined as a method of "testing multiple marketing scenarios and identifying the most promising for expansion."

Market testing, in layman's terms, is a method of determining how well a product, service, or offering will perform...or not.

Market testing is made up of research trials that seek to answer questions such as:

* How much demand is there for my product or service?
* Who exactly are my clients? What do customers think of my product or service in comparison to that of my competitor?

* What are my product or service's projected sales figures within a market?
* Where and how can customers purchase my product or service so that I can establish efficient distribution and marketing channels?
* What is the best price to charge?
* Who is my rival?
* Are there any legal impediments to the launch?
* Which sales, advertising, display, and promotion method(s) are most effective?
* Essentially, all of the concerns about how the market will react to the product's release.

The Difference Between Product Testing and Market Testing

Market testing is frequently confused with product testing. While it's easy to see why, there are a few differences to be aware of.

Product Testing

Product testing is all too familiar to researchers. The distinction here is that product testing entails observing a product's performance while collecting feedback from consumers. This entails using various research methodologies to collect data related to testing a product prototype with a sample of a target audience. Product testing is usually included in the development of any new product.

Market Testing

Market testing, on the other hand, is typically reserved for products whose performance is difficult to predict. It could also be used when product feedback is inconsistent or inconclusive. One significant distinction between market testing and product testing is that market testing does not involve consumer communication.

Various Market Testing Methods
Now that we've established the distinction between the two most common testing methods, let's look more closely at what market testing entails.

Close Response

Often, researchers will test the waters by asking friends and family if they would be interested in purchasing a product that addresses a specific need. Having those candid conversations is a great way to determine whether or not there is an interest, and if there is, whether or not it is large enough to drive purchasing.

This type of feedback is more casual. It could be a dinner conversation, a brainstorming session, or simply a sit-down. The goal isn't to collect conclusive data, but rather to see if there's potential (i.e. would people want it.)

Online Market Research

The internet is a vast network of resources that can assist researchers in gaining the knowledge they require to move forward with product ideas. Some of the best places to ask questions about a product idea are on social media, online forums, and online social groups. Furthermore, the internet has a plethora of other tools for market testing. Google Trends, Google Insights, and Google Keyword Planner are commonly used for SEO, but they can also be useful in determining whether or not customers are looking for similar products. Qualcast and Market Samurai are two common go-for to's information about the demographics of the consumers who would be most interested in your product.

Testing on a Small Scale

Small-scale testing is exactly that. A small soft launch to test how well a product performs in a small sample size. "If you're creating a physical product, have prototypes made so that people can test it out and give you feedback on its design and functionality," suggests Business Know-How. Alternatively, if you're developing a service, online business, or mobile app, create a simple, streamlined version and begin beta testing it, soliciting feedback on the interface, ease of use, and overall satisfaction. Take advantage of all of the feedback. Don't dismiss criticism without first considering it, and keep in mind that if multiple testers have the same complaint, it's most likely a problem worth addressing."

Small-scale testing also enables you to reduce risk. If a product fails to perform well in small-scale testing, you can go back to the drawing board without wasting a lot of money.

Competitive Analysis

Never be scared of competition. In fact, it can be a good indication that there is a market for your product idea. Plus, consumers like options, and who's to say your product won't be the best?

Your competitors are gold mines of market testing information. Examine the performance of their products for areas of opportunity. You can frequently discover flaws that you can exploit with your product. SWOT Analysis is one method for analyzing your competitors.

Market Testing Key Takeaways
Market testing is a method of testing the waters to see how well a product, service, or offering will perform...or not. It is typically composed of research trials designed to answer questions about how the market will react to the product launch.

Market testing differs from product testing in that product testing focuses on gaining feedback on how well a product is performing, whereas market testing aims to predict the market potential of a product concept.

Successful market testing entails employing a variety of techniques to produce a conclusive analysis of whether or not a product launch will be successful. Close feedback, online market testing, small-scale testing, and competitive analysis are among the most common.

The bottom line is that market testing is an effective tool for determining whether or not a product has a chance of success in the consumer market.

PART 5

MAKING SURE THAT THE PRICE IS RIGHT

Pricing is the most difficult marketing issue for managers. It's where they're under the most pressure to perform and have the least confidence that they're doing a good job. The pressure is heightened because most managers believe they have no control over price, which is determined by the market. Furthermore, pricing is frequently regarded as a difficult area in which to set goals and measure outcomes. When asked to define the goal of the company's manufacturing function, managers will cite a specific goal, such as output or cost. When you ask for a productivity measure, they will refer to cycle times. However, pricing is difficult to establish. Increased market share and increased unit sales sound promising. However, pricing is difficult to determine. High unit sales and increased market share may appear promising, but they could indicate that a price is too low. And lost profits are not recorded on anyone's scorecard. Indeed, judging pricing quality based on financial statement results is a risky business.

However, getting closer to the "right" price can have a significant impact. Even minor improvements can have a big impact. For a company with 8%

profit margins, a 1% increase in price realization (assuming constant unit sales volume) would increase the company's margin dollars by 12.5%. 1 As a result, even one step toward better pricing can be extremely valuable.

To improve a company's pricing capability, managers should first focus on the process rather than the outcome. The first question is not, what should the price be? but rather, have we addressed all of the factors that will determine the correct price? Pricing is more than just getting one key thing right. Proper pricing results from carefully and consistently managing a plethora of issues.

Based on my observations and participation in price setting in a variety of situations, I have identified two broad qualities of any effective pricing process, as well as a "to do" list for improving that process. Not every point will apply to every business, and some managers will need to supplement the checklist with additional actions that are relevant to their specific situation. However, by using these criteria as a guide, managers will begin to set prices that earn the company measurably higher returns, and they will gain control over the pricing function.

Coordination and Strategy

All successful pricing efforts share two characteristics: the policy complements the overall marketing strategy of the company, and the process is coordinated and holistic.

Strategy for Marketing

The pricing policy of a company sends a message to the market—it provides customers with an important sense of the company's philosophy. Think about Saturn Corporation (a wholly owned subsidiary of General Motors). The company wishes to convey to customers that it is friendly and easy to do business with. Part of this concept is communicated through initiatives such as inviting customers to the factory to see where the cars are manufactured and sponsoring evenings at the dealership that combine a social event with car maintenance training. However, Saturn's pricing policy also sends a strong message.

Eight Steps to Better Pricing

Fitting a pricing policy to a marketing strategy and considering relevant information in a coordinated manner are broad goals. The eight steps that follow deal with the essentials of setting the right price and then monitoring that decision to ensure that the benefits are long-term.

1. Determine the value your customers place on a product or service.

According to surveys, the most important factor in pricing for the majority of businesses is product cost. Determine the cost, apply the desired markup, and that is the price. The process begins within the organization and progresses to the marketplace.

However, in order to establish an effective pricing policy, that process must be reversed. Pricing managers must consider how customers will value the product before determining a price.

Managers must consider how customers will value the product before setting a price.

Consider how Glaxo launched its Zantac ulcer medication in the United States in 1983 to compete with SmithKline Beecham Corporation's Tagamet. Tagamet was introduced in 1977 and by 1983 had become the most popular ulcer medication and the best-selling drug in the world. Zantac, on the other hand, provided superior product performance: it had an easier dose schedule, fewer side effects, and it could be taken safely with many other drugs that were incompatible with Tagamet. As a result, its perceived value by the customer was extremely high. If Glaxo had allowed product cost to drive the price of Zantac, the medication could have been introduced at a lower price than Tagamet; it could have used a "follow the leader" pricing strategy. Glaxo, on the other hand, relied on Zantac's perceived value to the customer, initially pricing the drug at a 50% premium over Tagamet. Zantac became the market leader in four years. The pricing of Northern Telecom's highly successful Norstar telephone system demonstrates the same principle. As Northern's senior management developed the company's strategy for competing with Pacific Rim suppliers in

1988, they realized that the inherent superiority of their product didn't matter at first. Resellers would only value Norstar at the market price then charged by the majority of Northern's competitors. Rather than considering Norstar's costs and setting a price that may have been higher than competitors', Northern's managers decided to introduce the Norstar system at the current market level and then look inward to determine how they could reduce costs to make money at that price.

Northern's managers understood that they could persuade consumers that their system was superior to the competition's over time; in other words, they understood that Norstar's perceived value would rise as the system proved itself in the marketplace. Although the system entered the market at a lower price than it was worth, as Northern's competitors began to fight the commodity battle and lower their prices, Northern was able to maintain its price level, secure a price premium, improve margins as costs decreased, and increase its market share.

In Glaxo's case, a traditional "figure cost and markup" approach would have resulted in lost profits; in Northern's case, it would have resulted in a noncompetitive price and no sales. By flipping the process and allowing value as perceived by the customer to drive the process, each company found a better initial price level and the foundation for future growth.

Companies can assess the value that customers perceive a product or service to have in a variety of ways. Careful market research is one method; managers should also turn to employees who have direct customer contact, such as the sales force, for unfiltered information from outside sources.

2. Look for differences in how customers value the product.

A company can earn much higher profits by customizing prices than it could with a single product/single price policy, but many managers fail to recognize the benefits of customizing products and prices for different customer segments. A product's perceived value is often much higher for a "ideal" customer than for an average prospect. If this is the case, a company would be wise to divide the markets or segments and charge different prices for each. Consider how Polaroid Corporation introduced its SX-70 instant photography camera. Polaroid anticipated that some customers, such as those in the photo-identification card business, would place a high value on receiving pictures quickly and knowing whether or not the shots had turned out properly. As a result, the company segmented the market over time. To target customers who "couldn't wait" for the new product, Polaroid initially offered the SX-70 to dealers at a price of $120 per camera; end-user customers paid more than $200 on average. To capture a larger market, Polaroid offered the SX-

70 line at prices less than half of the initial level two years later.

The same principle applies in any business. Airlines, for example, try to differentiate between business and leisure travelers by offering lower fares with Saturday-night stay requirements to the latter. Companies can tailor pricing for segments that value the product differently by developing products with slightly different specifications from the same platform. Customizing prices is not only common; in some cases, it is critical to a company's financial health. Consider the magazine industry: When a customer purchases a subscription to a magazine, the cost per copy is significantly lower than the cost of a single copy purchased at a newsstand.

When software companies release a new version of a popular product, they offer discounted upgrade prices to customers who have already purchased the previous version. The manufacturers understand that the users' ability to continue using the old version of the product reduces their value of the new product compared to someone who does not have the product at all.

To some extent, simple differences in taste influence value variation; for example, some people prefer Big Bertha golf clubs to others. Managers, on the other hand, will be able to identify value variation and opportunities for price customization by answering the following questions:

* Do customers' levels of usage vary? Heavy users generally place a higher value on a product than light users, particularly in the realm of durable goods such as golf clubs, television sets, cameras, and so on. Heavy users may also be more interested in additional features or complementary products; ancillary products can be used as a mechanism for differential pricing.

* Do customers use the product differently? Some customers use a product differently than others, resulting in a difference in perceived value. Consider the coated air bubbles manufactured by Sealed Air Corporation, a supplier of protective packaging. The company recognized that viable substitutes for some

applications of the product were available on the market. However, for other applications, Sealed Air had a significant advantage; for example, its product provided superior cushioning for heavy items with long shipping cycles. Recognizing the extent of the advantages in various applications and understanding the value differential in each setting was critical to Sealed Air's product line expansion and pricing decisions. The insight aided the company's revenue growth from $88 million in 1980 to more than $500 million 15 years later.

The perceived value of a product varies greatly depending on its application. In many cases, businesses discover that a particular application for a product has a perceived value that is smoothly distributed around a mean. However, the mean for different applications can be quite different. Consider a computer manufacturer who sells similar workstations for two different applications: secretarial support and manufacturing design. (See the graph "Same Product, Different Value.") The average value of the secretarial application is significantly higher than the company's costs, but significantly lower than the value of the design application. In such cases, customized pricing can significantly boost profitability.

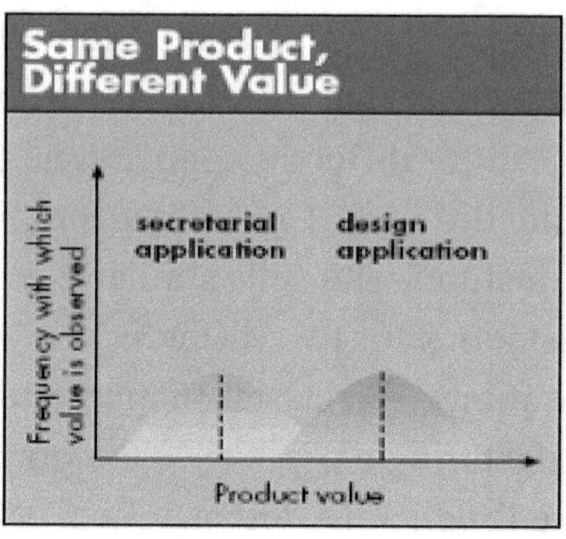

Same Product, Different Price

If markets are sufficiently large and show a variety of means, a company should tailor its prices. In some cases, customization can be accomplished without modifying the product. This is possible if no information about the product can be exchanged and the product cannot be resold between markets. For example, the computer will not be resold from the secretarial segment to the design segment. If information does flow between segments or if the product is resold from one segment to another, product customization is obviously required before prices can be customized. However, such an investment in different brand names, software preloads, or additional features may be well worth it.

* Do some customers value product performance more than others, even if the application is the same? Before being acquired by S.C. Johnson Wax Company, "Bugs" Burger Bug Killers guaranteed total pest elimination and charged ten times the industry standard because it targeted customers with high

failure costs, such as hotels and hospitals. "Bugs" Burger's guarantee of "zero pests" was far more valuable to those customers than it was to other potential accounts.

3. Determine your customers' price sensitivity.

Price elasticity, a key concept in economics, is defined as the percentage change in quantity sold in response to a 1% change in price. What happens if a company raises the price of a given product or service by 1%? On average, the answer is that the quantity will decrease by about 2%, but a "on average" answer is not very useful for managers trying to set prices. Elasticities vary greatly across product categories and even across brands within a category. As a result, companies must examine each individual situation. To measure elasticities, the most sophisticated pricing managers use market research procedures such as conjoint analysis, but a good first step is simply to examine the important factors influencing price sensitivity in three broad areas: customer economics, customer search and usage, and the competitive situation.

First, consider the economics of the customer. Price sensitivity rises, and a company's pricing latitude falls, to the extent that:

* Rather than a third party, the end user bears the cost. Until recently, pharmaceutical manufacturers, for example, had more pricing leeway

because neither the prescriber nor the patient paid the majority of the charges.

* The cost of the item accounts for a significant portion of a customer's total expenditure.

* The buyer is not the end user and sells a competitive product. Price pressure from the bottom of a distribution channel reverberates up the chain. One steel producer, for example, was able to achieve high margins by selling a component to buyers, who then manufactured specialty items for end users. Selling the same component to buyers who manufactured products for commodity-like markets resulted in lower realized prices: the buyers were more price sensitive.

* Buyers can judge quality without relying on price. Price has little impact

in difficult-to-judge categories like perfume because consumers assume that high price and high quality go hand in hand.

The search for and use of a product by a customer influences sensitivity to the extent that:
* Customers can easily compare the relative performance and price of alternatives. Consumers now have a better understanding of prices and access to alternative options thanks to advancements in information technology. This ability is likely to increase price sensitivity for a wide range of products and services over time. Currently, sophisticated businesses use information technology to track supplier prices on a global

scale. Consumers shopping at home via computer or interactive TV will soon be able to compare prices from a variety of suppliers.

* The consumer can take the time needed to locate and evaluate alternatives. For example, in an emergency, speed of delivery may be critical: price will not be the primary factor determining the purchase.

* The product is easily comparable. Cameras, for example, are easier to compare than computers.

* Buyers can switch from one supplier to another without incurring additional costs. In marketing its Quattro spreadsheet package, for example, Borland International emphasized its compatibility with and similarity to Lotus 1-2-3 in order to position itself as

an easy switch. This tactic increased the price sensitivity of Lotus 1-2-3.

Finally, in a competitive situation, a company's pricing latitude decreases to the extent that:

* There is little variation in the performance of products in the category. The consumer's focus is on minimizing the cost of this particular transaction, so a long-term relationship with the company and its reputation are unimportant. (See the table titled "Factors Influencing Price Sensitivity.")

4. Determine an optimal pricing structure.

Determining whether the company should price the individual components of a product or service or some "bundle" is critical. Should an amusement park operator charge admission to the park, a fee for each ride, or both? Should an entertainment service like HBO charge based on what it makes available or on how much viewers "consume"? Incorrect answers to these questions can be extremely costly. Most companies invest too little time, money, and effort in determining a pricing structure, and too much in determining pricing at different levels within a given structure.

When developing a pricing structure, two critical factors to consider are whether to offer quantity discounts and whether to offer bundle pricing. Quantity discounts are frequently offered in industrial selling situations. Consider a manufacturer who must develop a pricing policy given Buyer A and Buyer B, who value successive units of the product differently:

Units	Buyer A	Buyer B
1	$70	$70
2	$20	$50
3	$20	$40
4	$20	$35
5	$20	$30

For the sake of simplicity, assume that the seller is aware of these valuations and that one buyer will not resell the product to the other. The naive pricing manager would ask, What is the best price to charge? If the producer's cost is $20 per unit, the answer is $70. At this price, the company would sell one unit to each buyer for a total profit of $100. The astute pricing manager, on the other hand, inquires, What is the optimal pricing schedule? The key to understanding is in asking the right question. The optimal pricing schedule for the given cost and value parameters will be as follows:

buy 1-	$70
buy a second-	$50 additional
buy a third-	$40 additional
buy a fourth-	$35 additional
buy a fifth-	$30 additional

Buyer A would pay $70 for one unit, and Buyer B would pay $70, $50, $40, $35, and $30 for five units, for a total revenue of $295. Given the $20 cost of production, the profits on those transactions would total $175—a 75% higher margin than the naive pricing manager's optimal price of $70.

The second factor that managers should consider when developing a pricing structure is bundle pricing. For a manufacturer of complementary products, such as cameras and film, the strategy should be to forego some of the initial profit potential on the hardware in order to increase volume sold and, as a result, potential demand for software.

Aware managers can gain an additional advantage by considering appropriate product configurations. Astute managers can gain an additional advantage by taking proper product configurations into account. To be bundled, the two products do not need to have a camera-and-film relationship. Movie distributors frequently sell film packages rather than individual film rights because package values vary less across buyers than individual film values. Consider the following two films and their corresponding buyer value:

	Buyer A	Buyer B
Movie 1	$9,000	$5,000
Movie 2	$1,000	$5,000
Total	$10,000	$10,000

Buyer A and Buyer B both value the package of Movie 1 and Movie 2 at $10,000. If the company sells a package of Movies 1 and 2, it can charge $10,000, generating a total revenue of $20,000. If the movies are priced separately, the distributor would maximize revenue by selling Movie 1 to both buyers for $5,000 and Movie 2 to Buyer B only for $5,000. Thus, optimal à la carte pricing results in a profit of only $15,000. Is it better to price the bundle or the individual components? Profits are increased by 33.3%.

5. Consider the reactions of your competitors.

Pricing is more akin to chess than checkers. When competitors have had a chance to respond, a seemingly brilliant pricing move can turn out to be a foolish one. Poorly designed pricing actions, for example, can easily spark price wars. Pricing decisions must be viewed through a lens that allows for the consideration of second- and third-order effects.

Managers should consider how any price change will affect competitors. What are the competitor's initial thoughts after seeing the change? They should also think about what they would do if they were the competition. And, do I have an effective response to that action? Finally, they should consider the overall impact of the new price on the industry's profitability. Consider how Eastman Kodak Company handled its ongoing share loss in the US film market. In 1994, Kodak's market share of 70% was still the highest among industry leaders, but it was declining.

The company's flagship product, Kodak Gold, sold at a 17% premium to Fuji film. Kodak could have cut prices, but that would have been a costly move. Furthermore, such an action is unlikely to have achieved the goal of lowering the price premium over Fuji. Fuji, with a 55% gross margin on film, would almost certainly have matched any straight price cut to maintain industry relative prices. Instead, Kodak introduced a low-cost brand, Funtime film, in larger package sizes and limited quantities—priced lower than Fuji film per roll. Almost always, any pricing action taken by a company will elicit a response from a major competitor. American Airlines' shift to value pricing, for example, prompted nearly identical programs from Delta and United within days. R.J. Reynolds matched Philip Morris' price reduction on Marlboro cigarettes. However, competitors' reactions may not be limited to price changes; one company's price cut may prompt a response in advertising or another component of the marketing mix. So, if I cut my price by 5% in this product market, what price action will my competitor take? is only the beginning. A 5% price cut could elicit a response in a variety of ways. Southwest Airlines, for example, responded to American's value-pricing move not with a price increase of its own, but with an advertising campaign proclaiming, "We'd like to match their new fares, but that would necessitate raising our own."

6. Keep track of prices at the transaction level.

A company's total set of pricing terms and conditions for its various customers can be quite complex. They include early payment discounts, annual volume rebates, rebates based on prices charged to others, and negotiated discounts.

While a product has one list price, it may have a wide range of final prices, as M.V. Marn and R.L. Rosiello discuss in their article "Managing Price, Gaining Profits" (HBR, September-October 1992). Returns, damage claims, and special considerations given to specific customers can all have a significant impact on a product's real net revenue. Despite the fact that it is the "real" price (invoice plus any other factors) that pays the bills, most businesses spend 90% of their pricing efforts setting list figures. Treating the real price so casually can cost a company significant foregone profits, especially in a highly competitive market.

Price setters must assess and measure the bottom-line impact of the pricing program. The interaction of the various pricing terms and conditions must be managed as a whole.

7. Evaluate the emotional response of your customers.

Managers must consider the long-term effects of customers' emotional reactions as well as the short-term, economic outcome when analyzing how customers respond to a product's price. Every transaction has an impact on how a consumer perceives a company and how they talk about it with others. Quicken, Intuit's financial software, is priced at $35, and some believe that a moderate or even significant price increase would have no effect on unit sales in the short term. However, Intuit maintains this price because the vast majority of customers regard it as a "good deal." This perception has two beneficial effects. For one thing, it improves Intuit's reputation among its customers, paving the way for the introduction and sale of future products. Two, customers have become Intuit "apostles," telling others about how great the company is and why they, too, should buy the product. The pricing sacrifices some profits now in order to provide a significant benefit later on.

After you've defined your goals and needs, conduct some market research. Conduct online research or scout out local businesses to identify three to five main competitors in the industry. Whatever pricing strategy you use, what your competitors do will have an impact on your company's success and future decisions. Understanding your competitors' strategies can also help you differentiate your company from the competition. An effective pricing strategy can help you stand out in an economy where thousands of small businesses offer the same products and services.

Speaking with potential customers at the end of your research is a good way to get a sense of how they value your brand, product, or service. This can provide you with valuable insight into how to set your pricing. This type of research can range from casual conversations with friends and family to formal surveys of potential buyers. While you may have already done some of this research when developing your business plan, it's always a good idea to have as much insight and information as possible before deciding on a pricing strategy.

Pricing strategies to attract customers to your business

There are dozens of ways to price your products, and some may work better than others depending on the market you are in. Consider the following seven common customer-acquisition strategies used by many new businesses.

1. Price measuring

Skimming entails charging a high price when a product is first introduced and then gradually lowering the price as more competitors enter the market. This type of pricing is ideal for companies looking to expand into emerging markets. It allows companies to capitalize on early adopters and then undercut future competitors as they enter an already-developed market. A successful skimming strategy is heavily dependent on the market you wish to enter.

2. Pricing for Market Penetration

Price skimming is the polar opposite of market penetration pricing. You take over a market by undercutting your competitors, rather than starting high and gradually lowering prices. You raise your prices once you've established a loyal customer base. Many factors go into deciding on this strategy, such as your company's ability to take losses upfront in order to establish a strong foothold in a market. It is also essential to cultivate a loyal customer base, which may necessitate additional marketing and branding strategies.

3. Increased pricing

Premium pricing is reserved for businesses that manufacture high-quality goods and sell them to wealthy individuals. The key to this pricing strategy is to create a high-quality product that customers value. To appeal to the right type of consumer, you'll probably need to develop a "luxury" or "lifestyle" branding strategy.

If you've already started your business, you can try out these strategies to see what works best for you. You can also vary strategies between products based on the market for each good or service.

4. Economic pricing

An economy pricing strategy focuses on customers who want to save as much money as possible on whatever good or service they're purchasing. Walmart and Costco are excellent examples of economy pricing models.. Adopting an economy pricing model, like premium pricing, is dependent on your overhead costs and the overall value of your product.

5. Bundle pricing

Bundle pricing occurs when a company groups several products together and sells them for less than the sum of their individual prices. Bundle pricing is a good way to move a large amount of inventory quickly. Profits on low-value items must outweigh losses on high-value items included in a bundle for a successful bundle pricing strategy.

6. Pricing based on value

Premium pricing is similar to value-based pricing. A company's pricing in this model is based on how much the customer believes the product is worth. This pricing model is ideal for merchants who sell one-of-a-kind items rather than commodities.

How do you know what a customer thinks a product is worth? It's difficult to get an exact price, but certain marketing techniques can help you understand the customer's point of view. Request customer feedback during the product development phase, or hold a focus group. Investing in your brand can also assist you in increasing "perceived value" of your product.

7. Dynamic pricing

Dynamic pricing allows you to change the price of your items based on market demand at any time. Uber's surge pricing is an excellent example of dynamic pricing. During low seasons, Ubers can be a very affordable option. However, if a rainstorm strikes during morning rush hour, the price of an Uber will skyrocket due to increased demand. Smaller merchants can also do this, depending on seasonal demand for your product or service.

Which pricing strategy is best for you?

Each of these seven strategies has its own set of advantages and disadvantages. At the very least, you must ensure that your pricing strategy covers your costs and includes a profit margin. Determining your needs in advance can help you determine which strategies are best for your company.

If you've already started your business, you can try out these strategies to see what works best for you. You can also vary strategies between products based on the market for each good or service.

Focus on determining the appropriate cost range rather than a specific number. "Don't waste time debating $500 vs. $505, because it won't matter as much until you have a stronger foundation beneath you," says the author.

Regardless of the strategy you use, properly pricing your inventory is critical for long-term business success. You could have the best product in the world, an excellent team, and a stunning storefront, but if you can't effectively price your products, your sales will suffer.

PART 6

CREATING A BUSINESS INFRASTRUCTURE

A business infrastructure plan is a road map for starting and running a business. This road map is divided into three sections: daily operations, processes, and employees. Each component of the business infrastructure should be created and analyzed separately. The plan should serve as a stand-alone resource for how the company will grow and progress in the future.

The Business Structure

* 1. Choose a name for the business. If necessary, obtain a copyright for the company name.

* 2. Determine how your company will be organized. You can form a sole proprietorship, a partnership, a limited liability company (LLC), a corporation, a S corporation, or a non-profit organization. The requirements and business documents required to start a business vary by state.

* 3. Submit incorporation forms and fees to the state where the business will be located. Depending on how your business is formed and titled, the paperwork and fees required to form it vary by state.

* 4. Apply to the Internal Revenue Service for a tax identification number or an employee identification number.
* 5. Apply for a Dunn & Bradstreet number if your company will need funding or a line of credit from a financial institution.
* 6. Register with your state's department of taxation and obtain a sales tax license if you will be selling retail goods.

Creating a Business Plan
* 1. Research potential competitors in your area. Obtain an overview of the market and demographics in comparison to your business model, as well as a comparison of products and pricing. To obtain this information,

consult your local library, the Internet, and interview like-minded business owners.

* 2. Create a mission statement outlining business goals and growth projections. Outline what your new business will do, what you might need to start a new business, and what your business will bring to the community.

* 3. Specify the type of operating environment required by the company during its initial growth phase. Determine whether you will lease office space, buy existing real estate, or start construction on a new building.

Finance and Budget

* 1. Make a budget for your company. Start-up costs, salaries, operating costs,

and marketing costs should all be included in the budget. Detail the capital required to survive the first year, moving forward over the next five years from startup.

* 2. Specify what financial assistance is required to launch the business, as well as where the funding will come from.

* 3. Determine labor costs by calculating salaries or hourly rates for each position. Determine whether the position requires a full-time or part-time employee, a temporary hire, or a contractor.

Management

* 1. Create an organizational chart for the company, detailing the positions required to get started, from CEO and

management to general staff and hourly employees.

* 2. Develop job descriptions for each position. Outline specific responsibilities and who each position may report to. Rank each position according to need and budget.

* 3. Make a list of projected growth. Include any future employees as well as any materials or tools that may be required.

Business Infrastructure = Business Design + Business Process

A stable business infrastructure ensures the proper coordination of all human resources, processes, and other operational tools required to ensure manageable, profitable growth. This is especially important during periods of unexpected growth. Furthermore, business infrastructure provides businesses with:
* a solid foundation,
* a replicable platform,
* a model and a formula that makes each time you do something easier than the time before,

* consistency in your delivery of customer value, and economies of scale.

This is a time when size DOES NOT MATTER!

Every company, regardless of size, industry, or maturity, requires business infrastructure to answer the following questions:

1. What should be done?
2. Who is responsible for doing it?
3. How will we carry out our responsibilities?
4. What is the backup plan in case things don't go as planned?
5. How do we replicate our business model profitably?

Being able to articulate your business in a logical manner assures not only your customers, but also your employees, that you know what you're doing and that you're doing it in an organized and efficient manner. This translates into better customer experiences, which leads to increased sales. Increased sales necessitate the addition of more employees, larger/additional offices, and/or franchising opportunities.

PART 7

BRANDING YOUR BUSINESS

The branding of a company is more important than you might think. On the surface, your brand may appear to be made up of only logos and colors, but your brand is actually your company's entire identity. Your brand expresses your personality.

Business branding has always been important, and it may be more important now than ever. Every day, consumers are exposed to new brands thanks to social media. This is great for consumers who have a lot of options and can do research to find the best one, but it makes it difficult for businesses.

Because there is so much competition nowadays, businesses must go above and beyond to ensure they stand out. To accomplish this, you should invest in developing a strong brand that will capture and hold people's attention. You have the opportunity to gain some control over how people perceive your business with the right branding, so don't overlook it.

More People Will Be Aware of Your Company
One of the most obvious reasons that businesses require branding is to increase their visibility. People will

naturally take notice of your business if it has strong branding, much more so than if it does not. A company that lacks cohesive branding is unlikely to stick in the mind of a customer for long.

A company with a distinct logo, appealing colors, and other visual elements, on the other hand, will be much more memorable. Someone may only see your brand for a few seconds, but if it stands out in a positive way, there's a good chance they won't forget it, even if this person isn't yet ready to use your products or services. When they're ready to move forward, if your branding has stayed with them, they'll come back to you.

Branding Can Assist in the Development of Trust

Trust from your audience is one of the most important things you can have as a business, but it isn't always easy to obtain. People will be less likely to trust a company that lacks key branding elements.

Many of us expect to see branding when we look at businesses in any industry, and the absence of this could be a red flag for some. You have very little to show for your business if it lacks branding.

If you had to choose between a company with clear, professional-looking branding and one that hasn't made the effort, you probably know which one you'd trust more. Branding allows you to demonstrate to potential customers that you are a well-established, credible company. You can use this to tell people what they can expect from your company right away. This is an investment your company is making to improve itself, and potential customers will notice that you worked hard to create your brand.

It Can Improve Your Advertising
Without advertising, your company will struggle to get off the ground. Advertising and branding go hand in hand. If you want better advertising for your company, you must first work on developing a brand.

When advertising your business, you want everything to be consistent and to reflect your company's identity and values. This can be difficult if you haven't taken the time to develop your brand. If you advertise without strong branding, you're passing up a lot of great opportunities to create an effective campaign. Incorporating branding into your advertising will help increase brand recognition when everything is tied together.

It's Beneficial for Your Employees
Branding has value within your company as well. Of course, you want your employees to enjoy working for your company and to feel like they're part of a team. A company with strong branding will have an easier time

convincing employees that they are part of something bigger than their job.

In addition to branding that can help attract new customers, you should also invest in branding that keeps your team motivated. This includes small details like branded apparel and merchandise, as well as the overall appearance of your office space. If you can motivate your employees by creating a sense of unity through branding, you could end up seeing great results all around.

Branding increases customer loyalty. You don't just want customers who recognize your brand and use your business once; you want customers who return. You can give your brand a more human side with good branding, which your customers will relate to more than a company that is strictly all business. You can use branding to appeal to people's emotions and make them feel more connected to your company in a variety of ways. Branding enables you to build relationships with your target audience, which can result in them becoming loyal customers. You can create a brand that people care about and put yourself ahead of competitors who aren't doing so.

Branding is important because it not only creates a memorable impression on consumers, but it also informs your customers and clients about what to expect from your company. It is a method of distinguishing yourself from competitors and clarifying what you offer that makes you the better choice. Your brand is created to be a true representation of who you are as a company and how you want to be perceived.

Advertising, customer service, social responsibility, reputation, and visuals are all used to develop a brand. All of these elements (and many more) combine to form one distinct and (hopefully) eye-catching profile.

What is branding?

If branding were explained simply, there would be less ambiguity and dissonance surrounding the concept. Nonetheless, a solid understanding of branding necessitates a solid understanding of business, marketing, and even (human) relational fundamentals. Branding is such a vast concept that a correct definition that truly encompasses everything that it represents would not provide much clarity to the subject on its own. However, in order to reduce the spread of outdated, incorrect, and incomplete information about branding, we provide a more comprehensive definition:

Branding is the ongoing process of identifying, creating, and managing the assets and actions that shape a brand's perception in the minds of stakeholders. When comparing this definition to the official Cambridge definition, it is clear that the latter (Cambridge) provides more surface-level information, giving the reader a false sense of understanding. This could be one of the reasons why most people believe that definition is correct and use it to build their knowledge of the subject. In reality, basing your understanding of branding on a definition that reduces it to only one element (visual identity) causes every other branding-related concept to fall short when connecting the dots.

Our definition of branding, while seemingly more ambiguous than the other, makes much more sense when delving deeper into its meaning. Here's a rough breakdown:

1. Indefinite procedure

Branding is a never-ending process. People, markets, and businesses are constantly changing, and the brand must evolve to keep up.

2. Identify, create, and manage

Branding is a structured process in which you must first identify who/what you want to be to your stakeholders, create your brand strategy to position yourself accordingly, and then constantly manage everything that influences your positioning.

3. Total assets and actions

Your positioning must be translated into assets (such as visual identity, content, products, and advertisements) and actions (such as services, customer support, human relations, and experiences) that project it into the minds of your stakeholders, gradually building that perception.

4. A brand's perception

Reputation is another term for it. This is the mental association that a person (customer or not) has with your brand. The branding process has resulted in this perception (or lack thereof).

5. Stakeholders

Clients are not the only ones who form an impression of your brand in their minds. Potential clients, current customers, employees, shareholders, and business partners are all examples of stakeholders. Each person forms their own perception of the brand and interacts with it accordingly.

Why is branding so important?

Branding is critical to a business because of the overall impact it has on the company. Branding has the potential to change how people perceive your brand, drive new business, and increase brand value if done correctly or not at all.

"A good definition of brand strategy is the deliberate intent for the positive role a company wants to play in the lives of the people it serves and the communities around it."

Branding increases the worth of an enterprise.
When trying to generate future business, branding is essential, and a well-established brand can increase a company's value by giving it more clout in the industry. Because of its well-established position in the market, it is a more appealing investment opportunity.

The brand is the end result of the branding process, which includes the associated reputation and value. A strong reputation implies a strong brand, which translates into value. That value can be influenced, a price premium, or mindshare. The brand is a business asset that has monetary value in and of itself and must have its own line item on a company's balance sheet because it increases the company's overall worth. However this is a controversial subject and a difficult task for many businesses, giving financial weight to the brand is as important as branding itself - this is called 'brand valuation'.

Our 'Brands in the Boardroom' series makes an excellent point about the business side of branding.

Branding attracts new customers.
A strong brand will have no trouble generating referral business. Strong

branding generally indicates that consumers have a positive impression of the company and are more likely to do business with you due to the familiarity and assumed dependability of using a name they can trust. Once a brand is well-established, word of mouth will be the best and most effective advertising technique for the company.

The reputation of a brand, like the reputation of a person, precedes it. Once a market perception of a brand is established, an uncontrollable chain of propagation begins. Word of mouth will spread the perception and either reinforce or tarnish the brand's reputation. If the brand has a good reputation, potential new customers may come into contact with it and have an already positive association with it, making them more likely to buy from it rather than the competition.

Employee pride and satisfaction are increased.
When an employee works for a company that has a strong brand and truly believes in it, they will be more satisfied with their job and take greater pride in it. Working for a reputable and well-regarded brand makes working for that company more enjoyable and fulfilling.
As previously stated, a brand's stakeholders include not only customers but also employees. Employees are the

first line of communication for any brand - the first ambassadors - and human interaction is the foundation of commerce. Employees who have a positive association with the brand will spread that perception to the clients and partners with whom they interact. This can also lead to improved leadership, increased involvement, and improved products and services.

More information on the impact of branding on employees and the topic of employer branding can be found here.

The level of trust that clients can place in a brand ultimately determines its reputation. The more you trust a brand, the better your perception of it, and thus the brand's reputation.

Branding seeks the best way to establish and maintain trust between a company and its stakeholders. This is accomplished by developing a realistic and attainable promise that positions the brand in a specific market position and then delivering on that promise. Simply put, if the promise is kept, trust grows in the minds of stakeholders. Trust is especially important in crowded markets because it can mean the difference between intent (considering to buy) and action (making the purchase).

Branding in Activity

Branding is not a one-page topic. It is a constantly evolving subject that encompasses many areas of expertise, including business management, marketing, advertising, design, psychology, and others. Branding has several layers, each with its own meaning and structure. It is not the same as marketing, but there are many similarities between the two, which is why we cannot accept or deny that branding and marketing are somehow subordinate to one another. They are mutually dependent, and their primary goal is to serve the company.

Branding Mag's Roundtables are an excellent place to gain clarity and expertise on a variety of branding topics, including employer branding, country branding, brand design, brand governance, and brand valuation, to name a few.

"Brand" is more than a catchphrase or a company's fashion sense. It is a company's collective imagery, feeling, and reputation that follows it everywhere. When built correctly, your brand can help your company reach new heights of success. However, if your brand is built incorrectly, it may turn off customers and make profit impossible.

That is why it is critical to have a good marketing strategy and a solid understanding of brand management: what do you need for the branding process, and how does your brand image impact the customer experience?

This Guide will provide some branding guidelines and strategies for new entrepreneurs just starting out.

Branding is an essential component of any business, large or small, retail or B2B. An effective brand strategy gives you a significant advantage in increasingly competitive markets. But what exactly does the term "branding" mean? What impact does it have on a small business like yours?

Simply put, your brand is your customer's promise to them. It tells them what they can expect from your products and services and distinguishes your offering from your competitors'.

Your brand is formed by who you are, who you want to be, and who others perceive you to be.

Are you a trailblazer in your field? Or the experienced and dependable one?

Is your product the expensive, high-quality option, or the inexpensive, high-value option? You can't be both, and you can't be everything to everyone. Who you are should be influenced by what your target customers want and need from you.

Your logo is the foundation of your brand. Your brand is communicated through your website, packaging, and promotional materials, all of which should include your logo.

Brand Equity and Strategy

Your brand strategy describes how, what, where, when, and to whom you intend to communicate and deliver brand messages. The location of your advertisements is part of your brand strategy. Your brand strategy includes your distribution channels. Your brand strategy includes what you communicate visually and verbally.

Consistent, strategic branding leads to strong brand equity, which is the added value brought to your company's products or services that allows you to charge more for your brand than comparable, unbranded products. Coke vs. a generic soda is the most obvious example of this. Coca-Cola can charge more for its product because it has built a strong brand equity, and customers will pay that higher price.

Brand equity adds value in the form of perceived quality or emotional attachment. Nike, for example, associates its products with famous athletes in the hopes that customers will transfer their emotional attachment to the product from the athlete. Nike believes that it is not just the shoe's features that sell it.

Establishing Your Brand

Defining your brand is similar to a journey of self-discovery in business. It can be challenging, time-consuming, and unpleasant. It requires, at the very least, that you respond to the following questions:

* What is the mission of your business?
* What advantages and features do your products or services offer?
* What do your current customers and prospects think of your business?
* What characteristics do you want them to associate with your organization?

Carry out your research. Learn about your current and potential customers' needs, habits, and desires. And don't rely on your assumptions about what they think. Discover what they believe.

Your target audience is essentially the group of customers who are most likely to purchase something from your brand. You can narrow down your target audience by learning about its key characteristics, such as gender, age, location, and so on.

Conduct market research to identify your potential customer demographics. The more you know about your target audience, the better you'll be able to market to them and meet their needs in the long run.

Because defining your brand and developing a brand strategy can be difficult, consider utilizing the expertise of a nonprofit small-business advisory group or a Small Business Development Center.

How do you spread the word about your brand after you've defined it? Here are a few tried-and-true tips:

* Create an eye-catching logo. Put it everywhere.
* Make a list of your brand's messaging. What are the key messages you want to convey about your brand? Every employee should be aware of your brand's characteristics.
* Include your brand. Branding encompasses every aspect of your business, including how you answer the phone, what you or your salespeople wear on sales calls, your email signature, and everything else.
* Develop a "voice" for your business that reflects your brand. This voice should be used in all written communication and incorporated into all visual imagery, both online and offline. Is your brand approachable? Engage in conversation. Is it posh?

Make an effort to be more formal. You get the idea.

* Create a tagline. Create a statement that is memorable, meaningful, and concise, and that captures the essence of your brand.

* Create brand standards and templates for your marketing materials. Throughout, use the same color scheme, logo placement, and overall look and feel. You don't have to be fancy to be consistent.

* Maintain your brand's integrity. Customers will not return to you or refer you to others if you fail to deliver on your brand promise. Consistency should be maintained. I put this point last because it involves everything else and is the most important tip I can give

you. If you can't do this, your efforts to build a brand will fail.

Creating Your Brand's Style

Because your brand's visual identity can significantly increase brand recognition, having an interesting but distinct brand style is essential. Let's go over some of the topics mentioned above in greater detail.

For example, your brand's logo should be distinct, iconic, and relevant to your company's mission or products. Try to incorporate some aesthetic or stylistic element of what your brand does into the logo; if necessary, hire a good graphic designer to create a stellar logo from scratch.

You only have one chance to design a logo that your target audience will remember. If it's good, it will help your brand grow even more successfully. Logo design can help you attract new customers and persuade your target market/customer base to give your business a chance. Furthermore, it will be effective branding on product packaging!

Similarly, you should carefully select your brand's color, text fonts, and other stylistic elements. Depending on your industry, a specific color or text font can either attract or repel customers. For example, if you want to create a line of power tools for women, a red or violet color could be ideal, whereas pink might be considered too feminine for your target audience.

You should also consider how your brand's voice fits into your overall style. If you run a B2B company and primarily advertise and sell to others in your industry, for example, you should not speak down to them or use a lot of catchphrases.
Instead, use highly technical, informative language that demonstrates your brand's authority and knowledge in its niche. The opposite is true if you advertise and sell to the general public; the simpler and more understandable your copy and content, the better.

Spreading the Word - Maintaining Brand Consistency

Creating a good brand style is only the beginning. You must then ensure that you maintain brand consistency in all marketing materials you distribute, including those created by freelancers or third parties.

To that end, you should consider developing a brand style guide. All of the information above should be broken down in the style guide, including how your logo should look, the colors to use for marketing materials, and the brand voice to use for copy text.

Send the style guide to every marketing expert or professional on your team. This includes social media typography and messages, especially since you will often communicate with your loyal customers via social media.

The style guide must be followed at all times, including by members of your organization. Why?

The more consistent your brand feels in the minds of your customers, the easier it is to remember and the more memorable it will be overall. People are less likely to remember the name, let alone the purpose, of your brand when they need a product that you sell if it appears chaotic or disorganized. They may even believe you are rebranding or that your brand values are changing when they are not.

If you do this correctly, your brand will become synonymous with the services or products you provide.

Final Thoughts

Building a brand, in the end, necessitates practice, experience, and patience. Continue to iterate on your brand's identity and theme; as you learn more about your customers and what they want, you can tweak your brand until it is the most profitable version. Best of luck!

PART 8

BRANDING YOURSELF

Do you want to learn how to brand yourself? Creating a personal brand that helps you stand out in today's competitive job market is one of the best ways to articulate your skills, experience, knowledge, and overall worth.

"We are CEOs of our own companies: Me Inc.," management expert and author Tom Peters says. To be in business today, our most important job is to be the head marketer of a brand called You."

This article will go over 14 steps to successfully branding yourself.

Step 1: Determine your distinct value proposition.

Spend some time considering what sets you apart from your peers — your strengths, passions, and goals. What would your company and coworkers miss if you quit today? Understand who you are and who you are not.

Step 2: Determine how others perceive you.

Ask four or five trusted colleagues, coworkers, and friends to describe you in four or five adjectives.

What are your strongest points? What are your strongest points? In which areas do they regard you as "irreplaceable?"

Step 3: Determine your objectives

In six months, where would you like to be? A year? 5 years? 10 years? It is necessary to define your goals before you can create a message that will help you achieve them.

Step 4: Determine your target market.

You must define to whom you want to send your message, just as Starbucks does. This will not only help you fine-tune your message, but it will also assist you in delivering it to the appropriate audiences.

Step 5: Reorganize your priorities.

You're probably used to putting yourself behind your company, coworkers, and clients.
You still want to be loyal to these groups, but you must first be loyal to yourself.

Step 6: Pay attention to the details
Everything you do eventually contributes to your personal brand. Once your brand has been defined, make sure that the little things — how you dress, your body language, how you interact with coworkers, the emails you send — are consistent with your brand message.

Step 7: Revise your resume.

Examine your resume to see if it matches your brand. Make sure your resume accurately defines who you are and aligns with both your short-term and long-term objectives.

Step 8: Join a social networking site. Create accounts on social networking sites like Facebook and Twitter. Request that those in your target audience subscribe to your pages, which you should update on a daily basis. Make certain that your updates are relevant to your branding message.

Step 9: Create your own website. Your website should highlight your professional accomplishments, skills and knowledge, values, and overall worth. Make it about you, not your company or your clients.

Step 10: Blog

platforms such as WordPress and Joomla make promoting yourself to your target audience easier than ever. Commit to posting a couple of times per week on topics that will be interesting and educational to your audience while also highlighting your unique skills and experience.

Step 11: Get Published

Write a book, contribute to industry publications, or simply update the content on your own website. Being published is an excellent way to establish yourself as an expert in your field.

Step 12: Go offline

Make sure to promote your brand in person as well. Join and participate in industry groups, give talks at conferences, or offer to lead a large project that showcases your unique talents.

Step 13: Take care of your marketing network.

Keep coworkers, colleagues, clients, and friends up to date on your progress. Word of mouth is a powerful marketing tool, and what your network members say about you will eventually have an impact on your brand.

Step 14: Review your brand (and how you portray it) on a regular basis.
Are you branding yourself in a clear and understandable manner? Is your brand's message consistent across all channels? A periodic review will ensure that your message is clear.

Sold!
Creating a personal brand isn't an option if you want to be successful; it's a requirement. Whether you want to get that promotion or land your dream job, developing a compelling and consistent brand will help you achieve your objectives.

PART 9

SETTING UP YOUR WEBSITE

It is no longer possible to run a business, even a brick-and-mortar one, without a web presence. Consumers use the internet for everything from product research to location and operating hours. Even a simple, well-designed website can give you an advantage in your field, and if you have products to sell, your website can open up new markets and easily expand your business.

Website design software has evolved to make it simple for anyone to use. You don't need to know coding to create an appealing and functional website. Whatever program you use, you only need to follow some basic rules and tips to give your website a professional appearance, make it easy to find, and show your company in the best light

Your small business requires a website. Here's how to make one.

* Building a small business website is essential for informing your audience, explaining your value proposition, increasing brand recognition, and driving sales.
* To create a business website, you must first choose a domain name and secure web hosting. Then, optimize

your website to improve search engine rankings and drive traffic.

* Keep your website up to date and mobile-friendly. Also, make sure your site's speed is adequate to improve your search engine rankings.

* This article is for small business owners who want to build a website or improve an existing one.

1.Think about your specific user experience and the journey the user will take as they navigate your site," added Gabriel Shaoolian, CEO of website design and digital marketing agency Blue Fountain Media. "Whatever the fundamental goal of your website is or whatever the focus is, users should be able to easily achieve it, and the goal itself should be reinforced as users navigate throughout your site."

If you don't intend to accept payments (such as Apple Pay) through your website, you won't have as much work to do in setting it up. If you are a retailer or service provider and want to offer customers the option to pay online, you will need to use an external service to receive payments, which we will discuss later.

2. Select a domain name.

One of the most important aspects of your website is its domain name. It is the URL you will share with current and potential clients as well as promote on social media. As a result, you want it to be descriptive and simple to remember and type in. To avoid customer confusion, try to keep it short and avoid abbreviations, acronyms, and numbers. You must also choose your top-level domain, or TLD. This is the suffix that appears at the end of your domain name, such as.com,.net, or.biz. Nontraditional TLD names, on the other hand, have grown in popularity in recent years. These TLDs can be determined by geographic region, like.nyc, or on business type, like.marketing,.agency, or.law.

Once you've decided on a domain name, you'll need to check its availability and purchase it from a domain registrar. Here are some popular domain registrars:
* Domain.com
* Wix

* GoDaddy
* Squarespace

Check copyrights as you choose your new domain name to ensure that you are not infringing on anyone else's protected name.
If your preferred URL is already in use, you can contact the company that is using it and ask to purchase it from them, or you can use a domain buying service from a company like GoDaddy, which will contact the owners of your desired domain name. This service costs around $70 per domain.

3. Pick a web host.

Every website requires a host - a server where all of its data is stored for public access at all times. Because hosting your own website is likely too expensive for your small business, you'll need to use an external host. You have two options depending on your budget. The less expensive option, shared web hosting, entails sharing a server with other sites. Dedicated hosting is significantly more expensive, but it means you get your own private server and won't have to compete with other sites that could slow down your speed. Web hosting is included in some web builder platforms' monthly packages, such as Squarespace and Wix.

Here are some web hosting service options:

* **1&1 Ionos**: This web hosting company is well-known for its cloud hosting services, but it also provides other cloud-based services such as servers and site backup. Plans and capabilities vary, but pricing starts at $15 per month.

* **A2 Hosting**: A2 Hosting provides shared and dedicated hosting. For the first year, new customers can get a Lite hosting plan, which is adequate for some small businesses, for as little as $3.91 per month.

* **DreamHost**: DreamHost offers three managed WordPress hosting plans: DreamPress, DreamPress Plus, and DreamPress Pro. The average monthly cost is $16.95.

If you're looking for free website hosting, keep in mind that hosting a website is not free for the hosting company. As a result, they may use other methods, such as placing banner ads on your website, to compensate for the free hosting.

Consider how well a host can answer questions about its server locations and reliability, according to Jim Cowie, former chief scientist at cloud-based internet performance company Dyn.

"It's a good idea to ask, 'Can you show me how close you are to the major markets my customers will be in?'" Cowie said. "Any good hosting provider should be able to show you... performance metrics."

As your company grows, you may find that you need to upgrade to a different web host, or even work with multiple providers to handle your website traffic and operations. Cowie advised keeping a close eye on your site's performance and the experience your customers have with your website in order to determine your hosting requirements.

4. Construct your pages.

A good website is more than just a static homepage. Create multiple pages dedicated to different aspects of your business, such as a detailed catalog of your products or services or a blog section for company updates. In terms of your overall website, ensure that each page supports the site's primary goal, has a clear purpose, and includes a call to action (e.g., "learn more," "sign up," "contact us," or "buy this").

A contact page is one of the most important sections of a website because it is your customers' direct link to you, so include as much information as possible (your business's phone number, email address, and physical location, if you have one). An "about" page should also include information about the founding team or staff so that customers can put real names and faces to your brand.

If your company does not already have a logo, hire a graphic designer to create one for you to use on your website, business cards, and social media profiles. This will assist your clients in quickly and easily identifying your company on the web.

Justin Zalewski, director of product design at innovation consultancy Studio Science, shared a few basic guidelines for creating efficient, content-rich website pages:

* Be specific about what your company does. Lead with a clear, concise statement that summarizes what your company does. Within seconds of landing on your homepage, visitors should be able to understand what you do. A few well-written pages outperform dozens of poorly written ones.

* Place strategic calls to action. CTA buttons work best when they correspond to the information on the page. A "buy now" button, for example, makes sense on a product page, but a "contact us to learn more" button might be more appropriate on the "about us" page. Similarly, a page listing customer reviews could include a button that

directs the reader to the available plans and pricing.

* Improve speed by automating it. Set up as many automated speed improvements as you can. If you use a content management system (CMS), installing the right plugins will cache parts of your site so visitors don't have to download anything more than once. Zalewski recommended WP Super Cache or W3 Total Cache for WordPress users, which compress files and allow visitors to browse your site more quickly. If you are not particularly tech savvy, some of the more technical aspects of caching and compressing files may necessitate the assistance of a web development partner.

* Avoid using stock photos. The quickest way to turn a great site into a mediocre one is to use tacky stock photography. If you need photos for your page, it's best to use images of your actual team or office.

Pheil also stated that high-quality product images increase sales, so invest in good photos of the products or services you sell.

5. Set up your payment system (if applicable).

While this step will not apply to all business websites, companies that want to offer the option for customers to pay online must integrate electronic payment systems with their websites.

The simplest way to do this is to use e-commerce software or one of the best credit card processing solutions. Many web hosts provide an in-house shopping cart or integration with e-commerce programs. Conduct some research to ensure you get a solution that is simple to use and adaptable enough to meet your needs now and in the future.

Did you know?
Payment processing must be available on e-commerce sites, whether through their e-commerce software or a third-party processor.

6. Test and publish your website.

Before declaring your site live on the internet, ensure that it is compatible with all major browsers, including Internet Explorer, Microsoft Edge, Firefox, Safari, and Chrome. Examine each page and feature in each browser to ensure that images appear, links are correct, and the format is smooth. This will take some time, but the effort you put in now will save you future complaints from visitors who are unable to access certain features.

Additionally, ensure that your website displays properly on mobile devices such as smartphones and tablets. This step should not be overlooked, as Google and other search engines have shifted to mobile-first indexing, which prioritizes the performance of your website's mobile version when it comes to search engines ranking.

An analytics program is another essential feature to include from the start. By doing this before the website goes live, you can iron out any issues and coordinate a proper setup, according to Shaoolian. Once the website is live, you can monitor page performance and use analytics to determine why a particular page is successful or unsuccessful.

"You can examine any metrics such as city, browser, and so on to shed some light on how your audience is interacting with your site," Shaoolian said. "If you... implement this [after] the site goes live, you'll miss out on valuable data and won't be able to see which elements of your site are successful or unsuccessful right from the start."

7. Use social media to promote your website.

Social media platforms such as Facebook, Twitter, LinkedIn, and Pinterest are the best ways to expand your audience reach and inform customers about what's going on with your company. When you update your website, post about it on your social media channels, but balance it with genuine, non-promotional engagement. Include social media links on your website as well. The footer or ancillary bar are the most common places to do this (the extra menu in the top right that often holds login or contact links).

8. Invest in search engine optimization (SEO).

Submitting your website to major search engines, as well as implementing a strong SEO strategy throughout your site, will help direct potential leads to your page. According to Shaoolian, "defining title tags, meta descriptions, and Uniform Resource Identifiers (URIs) that are relevant to your company and aspects of your industry can boost your rankings in search engines for the products or services you're trying to market." Including relevant keywords in your content from the start, as well as a strong focus on SEO from the start, will help you generate traffic quickly.

These important on-site SEO tactics can help you improve your ability to move up the ranks as you build your business website. (You can also pursue off-site SEO tactics).

* Select the appropriate keywords. Choose keywords that are relevant to your company and that potential customers are looking for online. Visit our SEO small business tools guide to find a solution that can assist you in identifying, analyzing, and tracking these keywords.

* Publish new content. Regularly publishing on a blog, adding to your website, and updating your content all signal to search engines that your site is relevant for the chosen keywords. Choose topics that are relevant to your

business and exciting for your industry to position yourself and your company as thought leaders in the space.

* Insert internal and external links. Internal links are links on your website pages that lead to other pages on your site, whereas external links are links to other popular, high-authority websites. Place these links strategically throughout your website. Check that the links make sense, fit the context, and provide value to the reader; otherwise, linking may count against you.

* Image enhancement. Compress images so they don't take too long to load on your site. Take the same approach with video, ensuring that any clips load quickly and do not slow down the overall performance of your site. The metadata of images, such as tags

and captions, is another opportunity to work in your keywords and tell search engines about the images.

* Increase the speed of your website. Pages should load as quickly as possible; ideally, within a few seconds. To determine whether your site is performing optimally, use free site speed checkers such as Google's PageSpeed Insights.

9. Keep your website updated.

To keep visitors coming back to your website, update it frequently with blog posts on current industry events, new products and offers, and company news. You should also check your software and add-ons at least once a month to ensure they are up to date.

Even if your website host's security is strong, according to Pheil, if your software is out of date, it is vulnerable to hacking. If you don't have time, delegate the task to a trusted employee or a freelance website manager.

Creating a website for your company is a low-cost investment that can help you establish credibility and reach a larger customer base than traditional marketing techniques ever could. You'll never have to worry about "not existing" to your current and future clients if you keep your website updated with fresh, current content and are quick to address technical issues.

The Most Important Point

Maintain your website's fresh content and timely information to keep it professional and top of mind for your audience.

FAQs on business websites
What is the price of a business website?

According to Mark Brinker's research, the average cost of a small business website is between $4,000 and $10,000. The reason for such a wide range is due to the nature of the business and the amount of work the business owner is willing to do. The cost difference between taking your own photos and hiring a professional photographer can be hundreds of dollars. The same can be said for professional copywriting for web content and other similar projects.

How long does it take to develop a company website?
Website creation can take anywhere from a few days to several months, but for an average, we can turn to DreamHost, a leading web host provider for small businesses, who says the typical website building process takes between two and four months.

What information should your website include?

Every company should include pertinent information such as who they are, what they do, and how they can be contacted. Your website should also include the products or services you offer, as well as an easy way for customers to make online purchases. Businesses may want to include mission statements, reviews, and testimonials, as well as a regularly updated blog with useful information about the company and industry.

PART 10

GET THE ASSETS AND EQUIPMENT FOR THE LAUNCH

To be successful, your company will require unique assets and equipment. Determine which assets you require, how you will pay for them, and whether you should purchase government surplus.

Business assets are classified into three types: tangible, intangible, and intellectual property. You must decide whether to buy or lease assets for your business depending on the asset type. The first step is to determine which assets will help your business succeed.

Tangible assets
Buildings, vehicles, and equipment are used for regular business activity and lose value over time. Printer paper, for example, is not typically counted as an asset. When managing your finances, you can include tangible assets on your balance sheet as property or equipment.

Intangible assets
Intangible assets are things you can't touch, such as your company's reputation, brand, or influential network. These are not recorded on your balance sheet, and selling them for cash is often difficult or impossible.

They can, however, contribute to the overall value of your company.

Intellectual property

A type of intangible asset that includes trademarks, patents, logos, websites, domain names, and software. Copyright and trademark protection are frequently used to protect intellectual property.

Choose whether to rent or buy.

Once you've determined what assets your company requires, you can decide how to acquire them.

Lease

Leasing can be a good option if you need a large amount of equipment quickly or if the equipment is very expensive. You can also rent commercial space to run your business. In some cases, leasing is less expensive than purchasing with a high-interest loan.

Benefits of leasing include:

* Less upfront cash or credit required
* Short-term leases allow you to test out the equipment
* Maintenance is sometimes included at no extra cost
* Lease payments for business assets are typically tax deductible

Leasing has the following disadvantages:
* The lifetime cost is typically higher than buying;
* Replacing it when the lease term expires may be costly; and
* Leased asset depreciation is typically not tax deductible.

Every lease is different, so read the fine print of your offer to ensure you're getting something that works for you.

Confirm lease details

There are two types of leases: operating and capital. Because the accounting treatment differs, the type of lease you use can have a significant impact on your business taxes.

Operating lease

* Functions similarly to a traditional rental.
* Does not appear on your balance sheet
* Payments are considered operational expenses
* Low maintenance, risk, or tax obligations

Capital lease
* Works more like a loan
* You own the asset for accounting purposes
* Added to your balance sheet
* Claim depreciation and interest expenses
* Take on all maintenance, risk, and tax obligations

There are other factors to consider. Leases may include buyout options that allow you to fully own the asset at the end of the lease. A lease's length can vary, and shorter leases usually have higher monthly payments. If you want to break your lease early, you could face steep penalties.

You should consult with an attorney before signing a lease, especially if any of the terms or conditions are unclear.

Buy

Purchasing equipment can be a good option if you have enough cash or credit and are confident that you will use the assets for a long time.

Advantages of Purchasing:

* You can deduct depreciation on your taxes * Buying has a lower lifetime cost than leasing

* It can be recorded as an asset on your balance sheet

Disadvantages of purchasing:
* Requires more upfront cash or credit
* Less opportunity to "test out" the asset
* You may be fully responsible for maintenance and replacement

Purchase with cash or credit
When you buy assets with cash, you immediately own them in full. However, it also implies that you will have less cash available to cover operating expenses. Check that you've done your accounting homework and that you can afford to pay in cash. Loans can provide some of the same benefits as leases by spreading the total cost over a longer period of time.

However, you will pay more in fees and interest than if you purchased outright with cash.

To get more funding for your business, you may be able to leverage lines of credit with your bank or look for other sources.

Think about purchasing a government surplus.

Purchasing surplus goods from the government can be simple and inexpensive. Almost any tangible asset your business might require is sold by the government at or below market value.

When a federal or state agency has excess equipment, seized goods, or foreclosed property, it either transfers it to another government agency or sells it to the public. These items are sold "as is" through auction or negotiated sale online, in-person, or both. State governments typically have a single online auction site, whereas the federal government has several.

Start your search with this list of federal government auction sites:
* Surplus sales by state at USA.gov
* Military Surplus
* US Marshals Service - Seized Asset Information

PART 11

TURNING LEADS INTO SALES

What exactly is lead conversion?
Lead conversion is a marketing and sales process that entails converting leads into customers via nurturing tactics such as behavior automation, retargeting, and email nurturing. It is not to be confused with lead generation, which involves converting visitors and prospects into leads.

Before becoming a customer, a lead goes through several stages. They begin as a lead, progress to a marketing-qualified lead (MQL), and finally to a sales-qualified lead (SQL) (SQL). This means that brands must nurture leads at all stages and provide opportunities for them to take action toward becoming customers.

No two brands will have the same process because each will create a conversion path tailored to its leads. Below are some pointers for developing a lead generation strategy for your own company.

How to Create a Lead Conversion Process

* Gather lead information.
* Determine high-intent behaviors.
* Use a SLA to align your sales and marketing teams.
* Create the lead conversion path.

1. Obtain lead information

Begin with the data you have on your leads: source, industry, company, employee size, pain points - any information that will help you build a strategy that meets the needs of your leads.

Please remind me to trademark "leads' needs" after I finish writing this article. Now, on to the important stuff.

"You will waste a lot of time developing a conversion strategy that is not based on facts about your audience," says Marwa Greaves, Director of Global Messaging at HubSpot.

"Consider where your leads are coming from.. Are your leads most interested in your newsletter? Your website? On messaging platforms? Make sure you meet your audience where they are rather than expecting them to bend to your strategies."

"Understand why these leads are visiting your website in the first place. What is the underlying issue they are attempting to resolve? "You'll be much more likely to connect with them and convert them into a new customer if you can create email nurturing to help them solve that challenge."

If you don't have that information, work on gathering it through forms and user research. You can then create a customized conversion process.

2. Identify high-intent behaviors at each stage.

How do you know when a lead is ready to buy? What behaviors will the lead display? Having these answers is critical for distinguishing between leads who are ready to buy and those who aren't.

A lead who only reads your brand's blog posts is unlikely to be at the same purchase readiness as a lead who visits your pricing page. As a result, if you send an unqualified lead to the sales team, they will almost certainly have a much more difficult time closing a sale. How do you avoid this? Work with your sales team to determine what behaviors indicate low and high intent. Specifying those behaviors allows marketers to know what actions to take next.

3. Use a SLA to bring your sales and marketing teams together.

A lead conversion strategy will struggle greatly if sales and marketing are not aligned. A handoff cadence that works for both teams is one thing you'll need to agree on. This is where a service level agreement (SLA) comes into play. It is typically used to outline a contract between a company and a customer. However, it is also used internally by sales and marketing teams to improve lead conversion strategy alignment. Q1 suggests that an internal SLA include each team's goals, initiatives, and accountability measures for a specific time frame. However, as the business's priorities shift, this agreement will require regular updates.

4. Create the lead conversion path. Consider your lead conversion path to be a trail of breadcrumbs guiding your leads to purchase. The path itself will include offers and calls to action to provide conversion opportunities.

Example of Lead Conversion Strategy

As an example, consider Zion, a fictitious UK SaaS firm. The Zion sales and marketing teams collaborated on a SLA that includes the following: Marketing commits to sending 100 qualified leads to the sales team each month, and the sales team commits to following up with those leads within a week of receiving them.

Both teams have also identified high-intent behaviors that will result in automated emails and have put in place a lead scoring system. For example, if a lead achieves a score of 95, an email sequence is automatically triggered inviting the lead to schedule a product demo with a sales rep.

On the back end, that sales rep will receive a notification with information about the lead, their activity, and a timeline for follow-up. If the lead does not take action within a certain amount of time, an automated, personalized email will be sent to the lead on the sales rep's behalf.

This is an example of a path Zion can create to convert leads, both on the front end for customers and on the back end for sales and marketing.

How to Calculate Lead Conversion

It is easy to calculate your lead conversion rate: Take your total number of conversions, divide it by your total number of leads, and multiply by 100. This is your LCR.

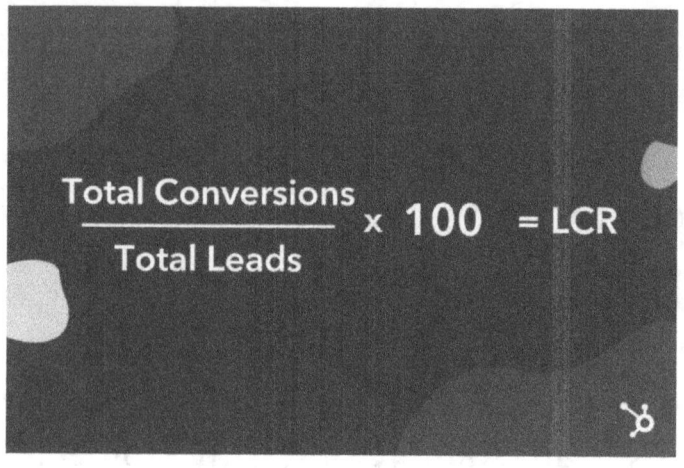

Let's say you generated 105 qualified leads from January to February. Twenty of those leads turned into customers. The formula will be as follows: 20/105 x 100. This means that the monthly lead conversion rate was 19.04%.

Lead Conversion Rates on Average

Because lead conversion occurs at multiple stages and across multiple touchpoints, no single average can be applied across industries.

Your brand would benefit more from examining conversion rates at a finer level, such as by channel (email conversion versus landing page conversion) and/or stage (i.e., MQL-to-SQL rate).

Lead Conversion Techniques
1. Introducing behavior automation.

Automation is useful for two reasons: it saves time and scales well.

Assume a lead is browsing your website's testimonials. This could indicate a desire for your product. With this in mind, why not automate a follow-up email that could move the lead closer to making a purchase? It could be a free trial offer or a product demonstration.

Emails based on behavior outperform other types of automated emails. Greaves, on the other hand, encourages brands to broaden their perspective when defining behaviors that indicate purchase readiness.

"Marketers should use activity-based triggers without hesitation, but think outside the box when designing them." Greaves says. "An automated follow-up may be required not only for views on your pricing page, but also for views on other customer stories or reviews on your site."

The following are some examples of behaviors that could benefit from automation. The protagonist:
* Examines your pricing page
* Schedules a product demo
* Signs up for a free trial
* Frequently engages in email marketing
* Requests information about product features via chatbot, email, or other channels

* Downloads a high-intent content offer
* Working with your sales team to identify key behaviors will aid in automating follow-ups that convert.

2. Nurture your leads via email.

Email nurturing is the process of engaging your leads through email marketing with the ultimate goal of converting them into customers. Offering relevant and valuable information is essential when nurturing leads via email.

This is where the data comes in handy. Using the information you've gathered on your leads, you can deliver content that piques their interest, aligns with their goals, and solves their problems.

Here are a few pointers to make your emails stand out:
* Add the lead's name to your emails.
* Use automation software to set up actions based on email engagement.
* Divide your email list into sections.

3. Make use of social proof.
When leads are thinking about purchasing your products or services, social proof can help nudge them in the right direction. Customer testimonials and reviews are examples of social proof because they provide leads with insight into previous customers' experiences with your brand.
They are most effective when leads are in (or near) the decision-making stage. As a result, you'll frequently see them on landing pages and pricing pages.

User-generated content is another great way to incorporate social proof into your social media and email marketing content.

4. Use lead scoring.

Lead scoring can aid in the alignment of your sales and marketing teams on MQLs and SQLs.

Lead scoring works by assigning points to lead actions and assisting marketers in determining where a lead falls in the funnel. It also assists sales reps in prioritizing leads and determining which follow-up actions to take. It also ensures that both teams qualify leads in the same way.

A well-qualified lead is one who is more likely to convert once they reach your sales team.

5. Retarget via PPC.

Retargeting is an excellent way to reach leads who have previously considered your brand but have not yet made a purchase. When you retarget them, you can reintroduce offers that they may be interested in or present new ones that are more relevant to their interests. Retargeting is a tried-and-true method of generating leads. According to Greaves, it can also be used to convert leads into qualified leads. With the latest restrictions on cookies, which are commonly used for retargeting ads, brands will have to rely more on first-party data for their retargeting efforts. Let's go over some other ways you can generate more leads.

How to Boost Lead Conversion

* Begin with the analytics/Start with the analytics.
* Define what high-intent behavior looks like in your organization.
* Play around with the conversion path. Lead nurturing workflows should be automated.

1. Begin with the analytics.

If your lead conversion rate is low, your first step should be to examine your analytics. Specifically, look at your conversion path over a long period of time to see if the low rate has been consistent or is new.

If it's the latter, narrow down the time period when the dip began and look for possible causes. If it's been consistent, you may need to experiment with your conversion path.

Greaves suggests examining your conversion CTA placements and the differences between them. You'll want to look for the distinction between high-performing and low-performing CTAs. If there are steep drop-offs on specific pages, this could indicate form friction, such as the length or order of the fields, or even the type of information requested.

If data shows that leads drop off shortly after being passed on to the sales team, marketing may have over-promised on what they could deliver.

With so many possible causes, begin with data to point you in the right direction. The pun was intended.

2. Define what high-intent behavior entails for your business.

Many brands may have lead qualification issues without even realizing it. Marketing may send leads to their sales team only to discover that those leads aren't ready for sales engagement.

How do you find the leads who are ready? It all starts with gathering the necessary information. To begin, contact your sales team to determine what information needs to be gathered. Then, compile a comprehensive list of high-intent and low-intent behaviors that will be used by the marketing team to segment leads.

This procedure can help you send more qualified leads to your sales team and increase your conversion rate.

3. Exercise with the conversion path.. Consider your lead conversion path as a house. "Why not use a road metaphor?" You could be thinking. But bear with me for a second. There will always be room for improvement no matter what condition your house is in when you buy it. Things to get rid of, fix, add, and redesign. And as your tastes change, so will the appearance of your home.

The same is true for your path. There will always be opportunities to improve your path. Furthermore, your leaders' interests, goals, and decision-making processes may shift over time, necessitating a different approach.

"Lead conversion necessitates extensive testing. You will not succeed if you devise one strategy and then abandon it "Greaves explains. "Developing an experimentation process that allows you to test every component of your flywheel will allow you to learn more about your leads and your own internal process than you would have previously."

Although the work is never finished, each experiment you conduct will bring you one step closer to converting your leads.

4. Lead nurturing workflows should be automated.

When it comes to scaling your lead nurturing process, automation is the name of the game. Manually sending personalized emails to your leads may have worked in the beginning, but it will quickly become overwhelming as your business grows.

Automation allows you to maintain the same level of personalization while spending a quarter of the time and resources. After you've established your conversion path, automate the follow-ups that will be triggered when leads exhibit certain behaviors.

These strategies will not only save your team time, but will also streamline the conversion process, ensuring that no leads fall through the cracks. This practice also frees up time for your sales and marketing teams to focus on high-ticket items.

The key takeaway here is that lead conversion is not a one-and-done process. It necessitates strategy, cross-team collaboration, and a great deal of experimentation.

PART 12

NETWORKING

Networking is defined as the development and use of contacts made in business for purposes other than the reason for the initial contact. A sales representative, for example, may ask a customer for the names of others who might be interested in his product.

To begin, the term networking in entrepreneurship refers to the creation and maintenance of social contacts that can assist businesses in meeting their needs. Nowadays, one of the most important things for entrepreneurs to consider is how to strengthen their networks. Furthermore, it has been said that who you know in business is everything.

Introduction

Businesses and business owners are involved in a wide range of social relationships, ranging from formal inter-organizational networks to informal networks such as partnerships and family ties, all of which influence decision-making and business efficiency. Furthermore, social networks accelerate business growth by lowering transaction costs, creating market opportunities, and generating knowledge spillovers.

According to a study conducted by the Economist Intelligence Unit (EIU), networking is critical for the success of 78% of startups (Economist Intelligence Unit, 2016).

What is the significance of Networking?

To begin, we will emphasize the importance of networking in entrepreneurship. Without a doubt, networking is one of the most valuable skills you can learn to help your business succeed. It takes a lot of time and effort to build a successful company, so it makes sense to have a network of business partners and associates to draw energy from and keep you motivated. Furthermore, connecting with others who share your enthusiasm and approach to achieving goals increases your chances of success. Furthermore, business networking is a great way to broaden your skills, learn from the successes of others, gain new customers, and spread the word about your company.

As a result, here are the five most significant advantages of business networking:
1. Possibilities
2. Guidance
3. New enterprise
4. Increasing your personal profile
5. Friendship
In other words, entrepreneurship networking can help your business grow and succeed

How to Expand Your Entrepreneur Network

Don't be concerned if your entrepreneurial network isn't where you want it to be. Instead, as you grow, you should always be expanding and improving your network, as networking is likely to never stop. However, if you want to focus on improving and developing the network sooner rather than later, here are some pointers to get you started.

You should participate in online communities as well as get involved in your local community. Participate in various social events and be prepared by having business cards on hand to hand out to others. Simply put, talk to everyone.

Networking entails making and maintaining contacts and relationships with others. Personal networks, both social and professional, can be a valuable resource. This applies whether you are an entrepreneur looking to start and grow your own new venture, a job seeker, or working on a project where external ideas and input can help. For entrepreneurs, a contact made at a purely social event may eventually help to provide you with one of the key ingredients for the start-up of the business.

There are several different types of networks from which to choose:

The social network

Your own informal network of contacts formed through social or non-business activities. These contacts could include family, friends, former coworkers, university contacts, and so on.

The business network

Contacts made through business activities, such as accountants and lawyers.

Artificial networks

The networks formed within business communities that are open to new members, trade associations, professional institutions, and so on.

Cambridge's business community has a number of local networks, many of which are focused on high technology and/or start-up companies.

Here are some general sites where you can network with other people:
* LinkedIn
* Facebook
* Twitter
* Cambridge Network
* Capital Enterprise
* Entrepreneurs Organization

Conclusion

To summarize, there are undoubtedly numerous benefits to networking. As a result, entrepreneurship networks are a strategy for small business survival and success. Thus, in order to be a successful entrepreneur, you must build a diverse network for yourself. Additionally, in order to establish a successful new business, you must establish relationships with those who you believe can assist you in achieving better results. Finally, we should mention that the larger the network, the better the results.

PART 13

GROWING YOUR BUSINESS WITH SOCIAL MEDIA

Strategic social media marketing is essential for small businesses. While large corporations have the advantage of dedicated resources and time, small businesses must be more agile, nimble, and creative.

It is not enough to simply throw money at a problem and hope for the best. You must be strategic in your use of social media to reach your target audience. Here are all of the social media marketing tips you'll need in 2023 to market your small business.

What are the benefits of using social media for your small business?

You've probably spent time researching social media marketing for small businesses if you own a business. With good reason.

There are now 4.2 billion social media users worldwide. That's nearly double the number from just five years ago, in 2017. Every day, these users spend an average of 2 hours and 25 minutes on social media.

Furthermore, social media is no longer limited to large corporations. In fact, 71% of small-to-medium-sized businesses market themselves on social media, with 52% posting once per day. You must go online if you want to compete.

Here are the top five reasons to use social media for business.

Reach out to more potential customers.

Every business owner understands how difficult it is to acquire new customers. You can spend hours creating the perfect product and designing an eye-catching website, but it will all be for naught if no one knows you exist. Social media has leveled the playing field, allowing small businesses to compete for attention with larger corporations. You can reach a larger audience and encourage them to buy from your brand by using social media platforms to create interesting and engaging content.

Increase brand awareness.
A well-executed social media marketing strategy will increase your company's visibility. People will share your interesting, relevant content with their followers, increasing your reach and exposure. The more your brand is visible online, the more likely it is that people will become acquainted with it and eventually make a purchase.

Better understanding of your customers

How well do you know your customers? While you may be aware of their demographics, social media can help you learn more about their interests, needs, behaviors, and desires. This valuable customer data can be used to improve your social media marketing strategy and ensure that your content appeals to your target market.

For each of the major social networks, we've compiled demographic data. Use it to determine where your target audience spends their online time. However, keep in mind that these statistics are only an overview.

Improve your understanding of your competitors.

Your rivals are online. Period. And chances are, they've already thought about their social media presence. By looking at what they're doing, you can not only get some ideas for your own strategy, but you can also learn what works well for them and what doesn't. This competitor data is critical in developing a successful social media marketing strategy.

Conducting a competitive analysis can help you learn what works and what doesn't for other businesses like yours. Don't be afraid to look beyond your main competitors for inspiration, and draw inspiration from the success of businesses in all industries.

Build long-term relationships with your customers.

Social media is about more than just posting pretty pictures with clever captions. It is also about developing relationships with your customers. These are the people who will buy your products and services and tell their friends about you, so it's critical to cultivate these relationships. Showing that you care about your customers and their experience with your company will go a long way toward securing these relationships in the long run. And, as your fans share and like your content, you rise in the social algorithms and gain new, free exposure.

Remember that the average internet user has 8.4 social media accounts, so you can connect with them across multiple platforms for various purposes. You could, for example, use Facebook to grow your audience and generate leads, and Twitter to provide customer service.

Let's take a look at the advantages of each platform for small businesses below.

What are the most effective social media platforms for small businesses?

It's time to go online now that you know how to use social media for small businesses.

Don't make assumptions about where your audience spends their time as you begin researching the best platforms and tools to build your social media strategy.

If you're looking to reach Generation Z, your instincts may tell you to avoid Facebook in favor of Instagram and TikTok. However, data shows that nearly a quarter of Facebook users are between the ages of 18 and 24.

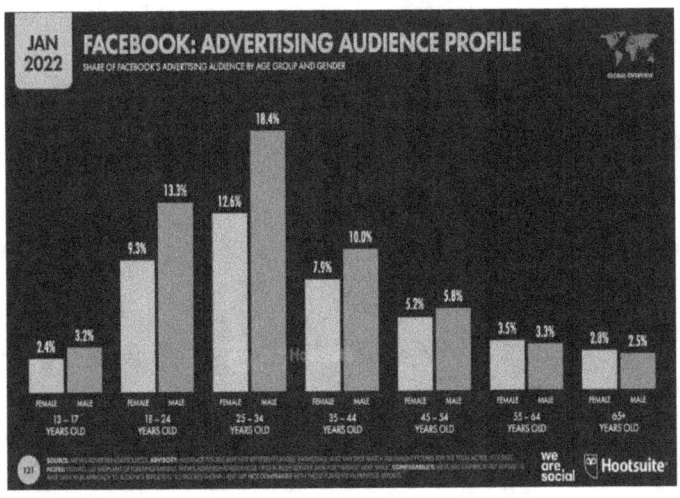

If you're selling to baby boomers, social media might not seem like a top priority. But it should be. For boomers, the most popular social networks are Facebook and Pinterest. Adults over the age of 65 are Facebook's fastest-growing audience segment.

Choosing your platforms does not have to be an all-or-nothing proposition. You can use various social channels to reach different audiences or to achieve various business objectives.

Here are the top social media platforms for small businesses.

Facebook

Whatever your feelings are about this social media behemoth, Facebook remains the most popular social media platform on the planet. It has over 2.9 billion monthly active users and over 200 million businesses.

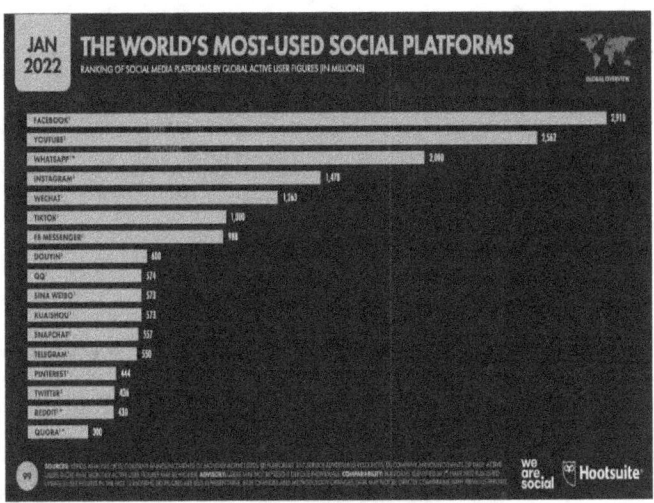

Facebook is an excellent platform for small businesses because:
* It has a diverse demographic. Facebook users are of all ages, genders, and interests.
* It has multiple applications. You can use one platform to create a Facebook page, run advertising campaigns across Meta products, track audience data, and set up an e-commerce shop.

* It can serve as a one-stop shop. Facebook can provide a complete customer service experience, from first contact to final sale.

If you're thinking about using Facebook for your small business, consider the following:

1. Who is your target audience? The most engaged Facebook audience is between the ages of 18 and 44. If your target audience is older than this, you may want to consider another platform.
2. What are your business plans? Facebook goals can range from increasing brand visibility through a Facebook Page to selling products through Shop or Facebook ad campaigns. Knowing your objectives

will help you decide whether Facebook is the right platform for your company.

3. How much time do you have available? According to research, posting 1-2 times per day is the most effective way to get results on Facebook. If you don't have time to devote to this, you should reconsider your resourcing strategy.

Instagram

While Facebook is a generalist platform, Instagram allows you to get specific about your niche. If you work in the fashion, food, or film industries, for example, chances are that the majority of your target audience is on Instagram.

It's also worth noting that the platform skews younger—the vast majority of users are between the ages of 18 and 34. If your target audience is baby boomers, you may want to redirect your efforts elsewhere.

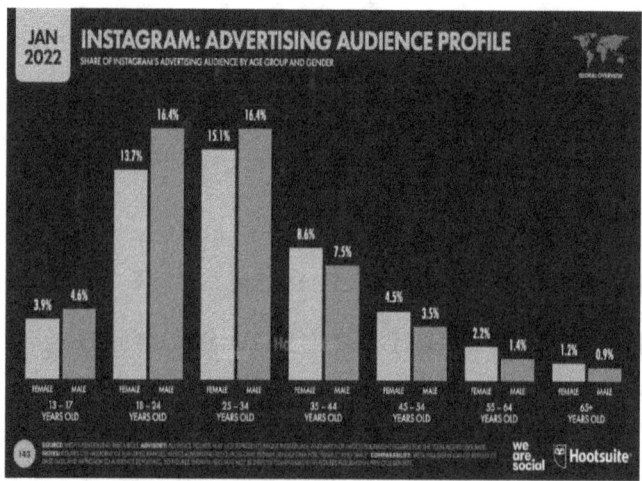

Instagram is an excellent platform for small businesses because:

* It provides in-app shopping. Instagram makes it simple for users to purchase products they see in your posts, Reels, and Stories.
* The platform is visually appealing, making it ideal for businesses in the fashion, beauty, travel, and food industries.
* Instagram users are active—the average user spends 11 hours per month on the app.

If you're thinking about using Instagram for your small business, consider the following:

1. Is my brand visually appealing? Because Instagram is a visual platform, your posts must be visually appealing.

2. Can I commit to posting on a regular basis? Instagram, like any other social media platform, necessitates a consistent presence. Instagram should be updated 3-7 times per week.

3. Do I have enough time to create interesting content? Instagram may not be the best platform for your business if you don't have the time or resources to create high-quality content.

Twitter

Twitter is another platform with a broad appeal. Twitter is the ninth most visited website in the world, with over 200 million daily active users. Twitter users are also highly engaged shoppers, with 16% of internet users aged 16-64 reporting that they use Twitter for brand research and 54% reporting that they are likely to purchase new products. Twitter has the lowest CPM of any of the major platforms for advertisers.

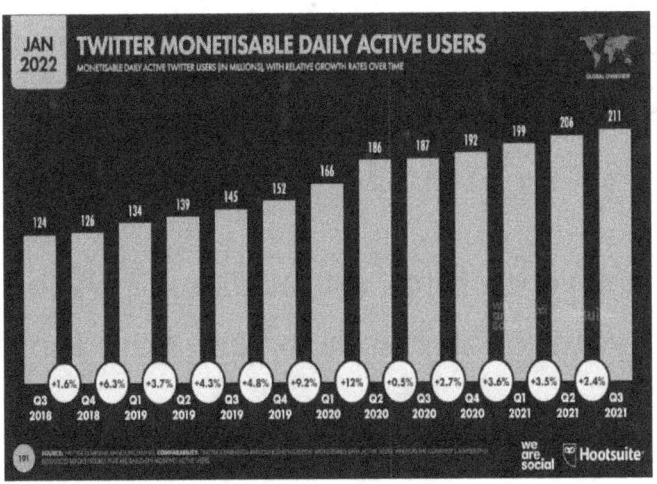

Twitter is an excellent platform for small businesses because it is:
* Conversational: Twitter is all about interacting with others. This can be

between you and your customers or between you and other companies.

* Real-time: People go to Twitter to find out what's going on right now.

* Hashtag-friendly: Hashtags are an excellent way to get your content in front of people who are interested in the subject matter.

If you're thinking about using Twitter for your small business, consider the following:

1. Do your customers use Twitter? Twitter is great for building relationships, but if your customers aren't on the platform, it might not be worth your time.

2. What kind of content do you intend to share? Twitter is a great platform for sharing quick news and updates, but if you're mostly posting images or longer-form content, you might be better off on another platform.

3. Do you have the resources to devote to Twitter? We recommend tweeting 1 to 5 times per day. If you do not believe you can make that commitment, Twitter may not be the best platform for your small business.

TikTok

Perhaps you believe TikTok marketing is not a good fit for your company. However, even well-known brands with audiences well beyond Generation Z are experimenting with this platform.

TikTok is an excellent platform for small businesses because it provides:
* A level playing field. A large budget is not required to create high-quality content.
* It all comes down to imagination. You'll do well on TikTok if you're creative and think outside the box.
* There is a lot of potential for virality. If your content is good, it has the potential to reach millions of people.

If you're thinking about using TikTok for your small business, consider the following:
1. Do you have enough time to make TikTok videos? While you don't need

an entire production team, creating TikTok videos and consistently posting takes time.

2. Is your target audience a TikTok user? Keep in mind that TikTok's audience tends to be between the ages of 18 and 24. TikTok is definitely worth considering if you're marketing to Gen Z or young millennials.

3. Do you have any creative video ideas? If you're not sure what kind of content would work well on TikTok, browse the app to get ideas.

Pinterest

Pinterest has evolved from a creative catalog platform to one of the internet's most powerful visual search engines in recent years. Pinterest users not only enjoy discovering and saving new ideas, but they are also increasingly utilizing the platform to make purchasing decisions.

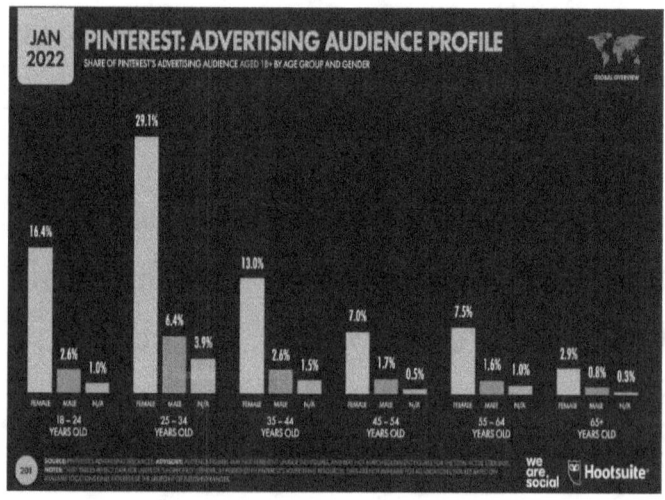

Pinterest is an excellent platform for small businesses because:
* It is a positive space. 8 out of 10 Pinterest users say the platform makes

them happy. Being present on a positive platform can improve the image and reputation of your brand.

* It's extremely visual. People enjoy images because 90% of information transmitted to the brain is visual. Pinterest is an excellent platform for sharing visually appealing images of your products or services.

* You can reach out to new people.. Because Pinterest is a visual search engine, you can be found by people who are actively looking for products and services like yours.

If you're considering using Pinterest for your small business, consider the following:

* Do you have enough visual content to use Pinterest? As previously stated, Pinterest is a highly visual platform. High-quality images will be required to make your pins stand out.
* Is your target audience on Pinterest? Women aged 25-34 account for 29.1% of the Pinterest ad audience, while men account for only 15.3%.
* Do you have any products to sell on Pinterest? 75% of weekly Pinterest users report that they are constantly shopping, so make sure you have something to offer them.

YouTube

YouTube is the most popular video-sharing social network in the world, with a potential ad reach of 2.56 billion people. YouTube not only has a large audience, but it is also an effective platform for promoting products and services.

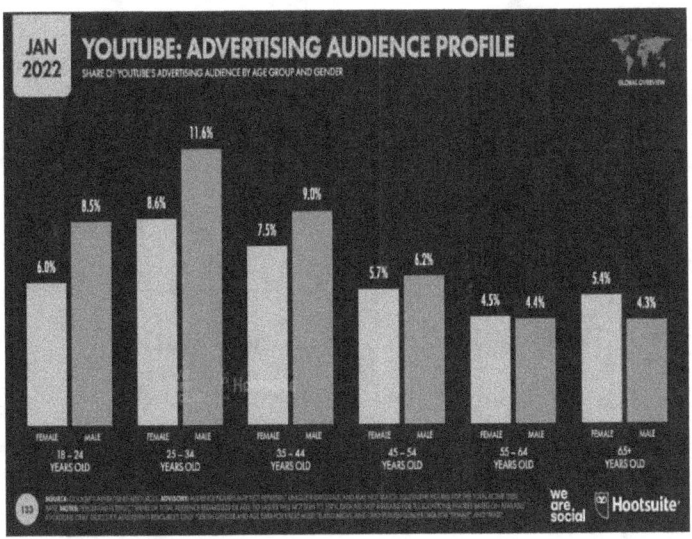

YouTube is an excellent platform for small businesses because it allows you to:

* Drive traffic to your website. You can drive traffic to your website by including a link to it in your YouTube videos.

* You can boost your SEO. YouTube videos frequently appear in Google search results, which can help your website's SEO. You can raise brand awareness. YouTube is a massive platform with a large number of active users. Use it to share engaging video content that will help raise brand awareness.

If you're thinking about using YouTube for your small business, consider the following:

1. Do you have the resources to devote to content creation? Unlike TikTok, making a YouTube video requires more than just taking a quick video with your phone. You should have a good camera and some editing skills (or access to someone who does).

2. Do you have anything unique to say? Because there is already a lot of content on YouTube, you should make sure you have something unique and interesting to say before starting a channel. Consider this: what can I provide that other companies in my industry do not?

3. Can you commit to a consistent upload schedule? When you start a YouTube channel, you must be willing to commit to uploading new videos on a regular basis. This could be done once a week.

Small business social media advice

Once you've identified the best platforms for your social media marketing, it's time to start posting.

To get you started, here are a few social media tips for business.

1. Prepare your content in advance.

The most common social media mistake made by small businesses is posting content on the fly. While it may appear easier to spend a little time each day thinking of something to post, this can actually be more time-consuming (and stressful) in the long run.

Creating a social media content calendar allows you to plan ahead of time and avoid last-minute scrambling. Furthermore, having some time to think about it makes it easier to come up with a mix of content (For example, blog posts, images, infographics, and so on.). When creating your content calendar, remember to include:

* The type of content you'll be posting (For example, blog posts, images, infographics, and so on.)
* The date you intend to publish it
* The social network you'll be posting to
* A link to the content (if applicable)
* A brief description of the content
* Copy to include in the post body

* Any campaigns, special holidays, or important dates to be aware of

2. Schedule your posts

Once you have that calendar in place, you can create your social posts ahead of time and use scheduling tools like Hootsuite to post them automatically at the appropriate time.

Scheduling your posts in advance allows you to devote one block of time per day or even per week to creating social content. It's far more effective than allowing social media to divert your attention away from other business tasks throughout the day.

Chatbots and AI content creation tools can also help you reduce the number of hours you spend on social media marketing.

3. Make a commitment to community management.

Yes, posting creative content is essential. However, if you want to see real results from social media marketing for small businesses, you must commit to community management.

Community management is the process of creating a community with your customers through online interactions. Responding to comments, answering questions, and interacting with customers on social media are all examples of this.

Consider it an extension of your customer service. You should interact with your audience just as much as they do with you. This way, you can build a customer base that feels connected to your brand and is more likely to become loyal, repeat customers.

Community management is also an important component of social media algorithm ranking. Platforms reward active and engaged users, so the more you interact with your audience, the more likely you will appear in their feeds.

Use Hootsuite Streams to interact with your target audience by liking, commenting, replying, and engaging with them. You can also use Hootsuite Inbox to keep track of all the conversations in which you need to participate so that you don't miss anything important.

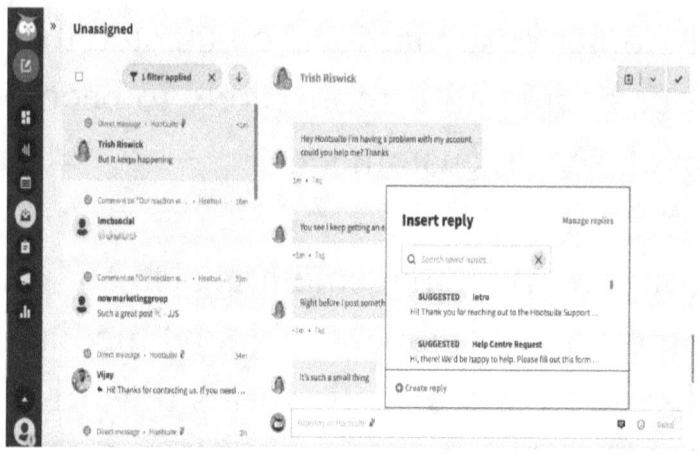

4. Pay attention to trends

We're not saying you should jump on every meme that goes viral. (In fact, don't jump on every viral meme.) However, it is a good idea to pay attention to social media trends so that you understand what people are looking for when they sign into their social channels. This enables you to create relevant content that will resonate over time.

If you have the time to devote to it, social listening is a highly valuable information-gathering tool that can help you understand what your audience (and potential audience) might want to hear from your business. It's extremely simple to do with a tool like Hootsuite. You can easily set up a stream for mentions of your brand on various social channels, allowing you to respond to concerns or positive reviews quickly and keep track of public opinion about your company.

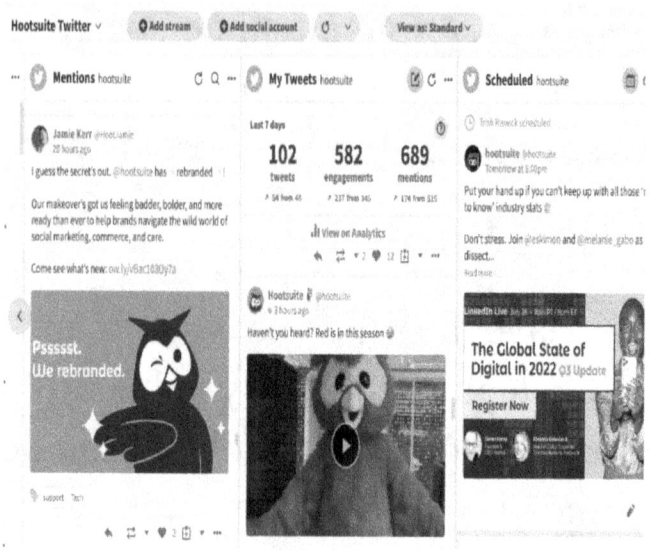

5. Promote products on social media.
In recent years, social media marketing
has evolved to include social
commerce: the ability to sell products
directly through social channels. And
business is booming, with a $492 billion
global market value projected in 2022.

Almost every social platform now has some sort of social selling capability. There are Shops on Facebook and Instagram, Buyable Pins on Pinterest, the TikTok Shop, and more.

Social commerce is an especially effective strategy for small businesses in the ecommerce or retail sectors. The beauty of it is that you can eliminate many of the stumbling blocks that come with selling online. Because your potential customers are already on social media, they don't need to visit your website and navigate to your product pages. And because you're meeting them where they are, you have a much better chance of closing the deal.

6. Use analytics to guide future posts

Even small businesses must keep track of what works and what doesn't on social media. Social media analytics tools can assist you in tracking your progress over time and determining which posts are generating the most engagement- likes, comments, shares, clicks, etc.

This data can be extremely useful as you plan future content. If you notice that a certain type of post is performing well, try to replicate that success in future posts. If you notice that a certain type of post isn't performing well, try experimenting with new content to see if you can find a better way to engage your audience.

Analytics can also assist you in determining which social media platform is most effective for your company. If you notice that one platform is receiving more engagement than another, you might want to consider switching. You don't have to be everywhere, so focus on the platforms that produce the best results for you.

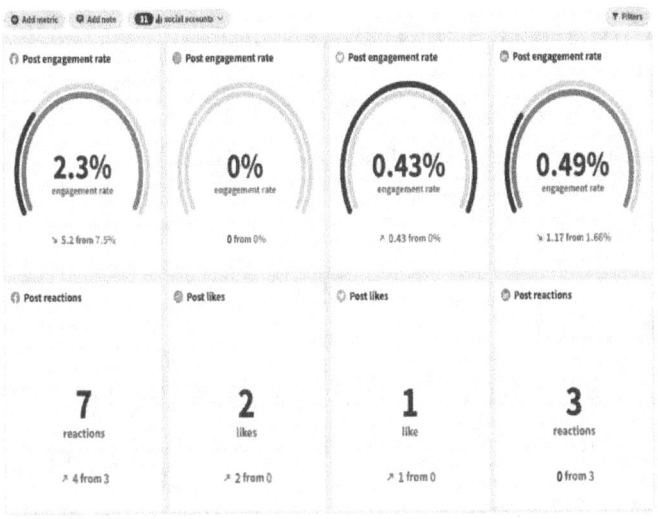

Small-business social media management software

If you're like the majority of small business owners, you wear many hats. You're the CEO, CFO, and sales superstar. It's no surprise that marketing is frequently neglected!

Even if you aren't a marketing expert, you can still effectively market your business on social media. In fact, using social media to reach your target audience can actually save you time and energy with the right tools.

Hootsuite

We're obviously biased, but we believe Hootsuite is especially beneficial to small business owners. Hootsuite is a social media management platform that allows you to track and post to all of your social media channels in one place, saving you a significant amount of time in the long run.

It also suggests when to post, what type of content to post, and how to interpret your performance. As a result, it's a beginner-friendly platform for those who don't have a lot of time to spend developing the perfect strategy.

PART 14

MARKETING YOUR GROWING BUSINESS

Your product or service is making consistent profits. That success may be slowing down in some cases. The last thing you want is for your marketing efforts to stagnate.

To keep your established business strong and healthy, alter your marketing strategy so that it evolves with your audience. If you do not change your approach during this stage, you may lose even your most loyal customers. Here's what you can do to market your business strategically and avoid revenue loss once it has reached maturity.

Determine how to win new clients. It's wise to do everything you can to keep your current customers. Nonetheless, even at this stage of maturity, you want to convert prospects into customers. You may be able to enter a new market or territory, or you may be able to win over the customers of a competitor by providing better service or value.

To reach out to new customers, you'll need to employ some of your previous marketing strategies. Your understanding of what these audiences want and how they prefer to interact with a brand should inform those tactics. You can't expect the same messaging and campaign approaches to work for prospects in different areas. If you're going after the competition's customer base, it's critical to differentiate your offer from theirs, and then emphasize that in your marketing. Find a compelling reason for the customers of the competition to switch brands.

All of this intelligence gathering could take a long time. However, it will be worthwhile if your marketing campaigns address the very things that all of these potential customers desire from a company.

Helpful Hint

With Jotform's free online marketing forms, you can collect email signups, surveys, and more.

Relaunch or revitalize a product or service

If your company is mature, chances are your products or services are as well. Perhaps it's time for a refresh to keep your offering appealing and relevant to current and prospective customers. Investigate new ways to use your product or service and make that the focal point of your marketing content. Enhancements may include increasing a product's durability, dependability, or overall performance. Focus your marketing efforts on demonstrating how you've improved the customer experience, such as through a better checkout system, new store decor or layout, or personalized shopping experiences, in the case of services.

Alternatively, you can add new features to meet the needs of your audience, such as increased safety, convenience, and even fun. This demonstrates that your brand is on the cutting edge of trends, including a keen understanding of what affects your target audience. Furthermore, new value-added features contribute to the creation of excitement and buzz during the shopping and purchasing experiences.

Conduct additional market research to inform any changes in strategy or messaging.

If you're not sure what to change or if you're feeling stuck in your market position, it's time to conduct external and internal research. This may help you identify what changes you need to make to get back on track.

Examine what's going on with your target audience, the competition, and external factors such as the economic and legal environments to get a better idea of how to change your strategy. Even auditing your internal environment can help you identify inefficiencies or areas that need to be changed to ensure your marketing is sending the correct message.

Examine your pricing strategy to see if a change is necessary.
Consider how to improve your marketing mix, as you would with any business cycle. At this point, you may want to consider whether price changes will keep customers coming back. Lowering prices may also attract new

customers who will leave the competition if they see you offer a better deal.

However, you may need to raise the price, especially if you make this change in conjunction with a product reintroduction. Raising the price allows you to differentiate your product from others on the market in terms of superior features, benefits, and quality. Marketing your product or service at a higher price point may also attract the attention of a new audience segment that's focused solely on high-end brands.

Marketing Cycles

In addition to the strategies listed above, you should think about the next steps in your business after it has reached maturity — that is, during the decline or exit stage. Perhaps an exit strategy is the best option, or you should rebrand the company or pivot into a new niche. During the maturity stage, it is critical to consider the next step you want to take because your marketing efforts should begin to reflect that decision. Recognizing that direction in your marketing can pave the way for the next stage, which could include attracting a buyer or acquisition candidate.

PART 15

REACHING NEW MARKETS AND OFFERING NEW PRODUCTS

Expansion into a new market entails growing your business by investigating related industries or niche product areas where you can succeed. The goal of entering a new market is to improve your company in one or more ways. Here are some reasons why businesses enter new markets:

* To compete: Businesses may benefit from expanding into new markets because it allows them to compete with

competing businesses that have already expanded their product lines.

* To expand one's customer base: When businesses want to expand their customer base, expanding into new markets allows them to connect with different target audiences who can benefit from their new products or services and existing product lines.

* To meet the growing needs of existing customers: When customers' needs change, businesses can expand into new markets to meet those needs while retaining their existing customer bases.

How to enter a new market

Examine the following steps to determine how to enter a new market as a business:

1. Examine your current business model and target audiences.

By reviewing your current business model, product or service offerings, and target audiences, you may be able to identify one or more areas for improvement. You can also review the types of solutions you provide to your customers and how you could improve them to improve their experiences.

For instance, the executive team of a major clothing retailer examines their company's original business model. The mission statement describes their goal of inspiring creativity and originality in a world of trends. Following further discussion, the executive team decides that any expansion into a new market will be aligned with their original company mission.

2. Consider your company's long-term goals.

The vision statement of your company can provide you with valuable insights into potential expansion areas. This is because you can identify a product market that will help your company achieve its objectives.

For instance, the vision statement of a clothing retailer is "To assist in displaying a person's inner creativity to the world." As a result, executives may decide to select products that allow them to continue bringing inner creativity outward.

3. Investigate competitor markets

Your competitors can also help you identify potential markets for expansion. You can do this by examining your top competitors' products or services and what they provide that distinguishes them from other companies in your industry. "Market analysts and marketing specialists at the clothing retailer spend time reviewing product offerings from other major retailers in their industry," for example. Three of the five major competitors have expanded into beauty and cosmetics, jewelry, and designer shoe lines, according to their findings.

4. Conduct thorough market research on related product markets

Complete market research for a few product markets to understand the types of products or services offered, the types of businesses involved, and the types of consumers who buy from them. This allows you to determine which markets will benefit your company the most.

Market analysts and other marketing professionals, for example, investigate related markets such as the beauty, jewelry, footwear, and home furnishings industries. They determine that the beauty, jewelry, and footwear industries have a high concentration of clothing retail businesses. However, there aren't as many clothing retailers expanding into the home furnishings industry.

5. Pick one target market to concentrate on.

After evaluating several markets for expansion, choose the one that best aligns with your company's current and future goals.

For example, based on market research, a clothing retailer decides to expand into the home furnishings market to assist customers in transferring their inner creativity to not only clothing, but also the way they decorate their living spaces.

6. Gather feedback from existing customer bases

Set up surveys for emails or website pop-ups that allow customers to select which products or services they want to see from your company next to determine customer perception. This can also help you confirm your new market choice.

For example, using email lists, the marketing team creates surveys to send out with website discounts for loyal customers who complete them. They include a list of products, including home furnishings, and ask customers which ones they want to see next. Because the majority of customers requested a home furnishing line, they decided to enter the home furnishings market.

7. Create a budget to enter a new market.

When preparing to enter a new market, you must first determine the amount of money available for expansion and other resource requirements. This can assist you in determining which activities you can afford to do right now and which you will need to budget for in the future.

Related: The clothing store determines that they currently have $500,000 in funds available for the purchase and sale of home decor items. They decide to postpone purchasing furniture because it requires more time and money than they can currently afford. Instead, they decide to sell the rugs, wall tapestries, candles, decorative light fixtures, pillows, throw blankets, and candles that are offered by quality wholesalers.

8. Establish a timetable for expanding into another market.

The timeframe for entering another market may be determined by your budget, manufacturing costs, hiring requirements, and marketing materials. In any case, by establishing a timetable, you create an end goal that will guide all expansion activities.

Planning and implementing a growth strategy to develop new markets and expand your business before your current market flattens out will not only help your business survive difficult times, but it may also provide you with a significant competitive advantage.

PART 16

GROWING YOUR BUSINESS
WITH WIN-WIN
RELATIONSHIPS

People, not contracts, create successful relationships. It necessitates the willingness to lay the groundwork for trust, loyalty, and commitment. Remember that every relationship is unique and should be treated as such. The basic rule is that you get out of a relationship what you put into it. A successful partnership is one in which everyone benefits. It replaces the old "us versus them" mentality with a new "us" that allows everyone to grow and reach their full potential.

People who are skilled at forming successful alliances work very hard to create win-win situations. In the long run, a partnership succeeds when both organizations work together for the common good rather than competing with each other. When partners spend all of their time trying to outnegotiate one another, everyone loses.

Furthermore, one of the organizations is likely to come out on top, causing jealousy and resentment. In win-win relationships, everyone does their best to understand and meet their partner's needs.

Previously, conventional wisdom held that having multiple vendors increased competition and improved performance; that pitting one supplier against another was good business. The goal was to win at any cost. Today, however, the trend is quite the opposite. Experience has shown that the only way to build long-lasting relationships is to start with good intentions, make a commitment, and invest time and effort in a select few.

What Causes the Failure of Business Relationships?

There is no single set of rules for success, but certain behaviors should be avoided. Partnerships, for example, cannot succeed if one partner is kept in the dark and is unaware of key events. Partnerships cannot succeed when one partner attempts to gain an advantage or has selfish motives. Furthermore, partnerships cannot succeed if scapegoating occurs; everyone should have a vested interest in the venture's success.

Relationships fail for a variety of reasons, the most important of which are:

Lack of dedication. Relationships fail when partners are not equally committed to the venture or to creating a win-win situation. As a result, one partner resents making a larger commitment and receiving little in return.

Cultural distinctions. When partners, particularly organizations, are unable to adapt their work styles to complement the other's culture, relationships fail. For example, an entrepreneurial organization that thrives on flexibility may struggle to collaborate with a large bureaucratic organization that requires several layers of approval before making decisions.

Poor management. Relationships fail because management does not value the relationship and makes the necessary personal investment to grow it. The relationship will not flourish unless management fully supports it.

Poor communication. Relationships fail when organizations obstruct the exchange of information. People spend their time looking over their shoulders rather than moving the venture forward unless there is an open and honest communication philosophy. Furthermore, the reasoning behind decisions may not be fully understood, resulting in errors, redundancies, and misunderstandings.

Individual relationship failure.
Relationships fail because the people in charge of them lack either the interpersonal skills or the personal chemistry required to nurture them.

Win-Win: We're a Team
Today's lean organizations cannot survive without strong alliances to supplement their core capabilities. As a result, we have entered a new era of collaboration, with unexpected benefits. However, cooperative arrangements entail responsibilities, both now and in the future.
Every partnership should go beyond the formal boundaries of a signed contract and be willing to do more than was originally planned. Partners should

promote the idea that the relationship was formed for the long term rather than for a specific purpose. This could include making investments that aren't immediately beneficial to your organization or assisting your partner in ways that aren't directly related to the relationship.

Business relationships do not just happen. They are the result of trust, confidence, and openness, as well as honesty, integrity, respect, and commitment. Partners in any healthy relationship foster an environment that promotes continuous improvement, risk taking, a long-term perspective, and, of course, win-win relationships. Obviously, the stronger these characteristics are, the more durable your partnerships will be.

PART 17

CREATING WORK-LIFE BALANCE

Balancing your professional and personal lives can be difficult, but it is essential.

Here's how to improve your work-life balance today.

Work frequently takes precedence over everything else in our lives. Our desire to succeed professionally can cause us to neglect our own well-being. Creating a harmonious work-life balance or work-life integration is critical, however, not only for our physical, emotional, and mental well-being, but also for our career.

What exactly is work-life balance, and why is it so important?
In a nutshell, work-life balance is a state of equilibrium in which a person prioritizes the demands of one's career and the demands of one's personal life equally. Some of the most common causes of a poor work-life balance are:
* Increased work responsibilities

* Working longer hours
* Increased home responsibilities
* Having children

According to Chris Chancey, career expert and CEO of Amplio Recruiting, a good work-life balance has numerous benefits, including less stress, a lower risk of burnout, and a greater sense of well-being. This benefits both employees and employers.

Employers who are committed to providing environments that promote work-life balance for their employees can save money, have fewer cases of absenteeism, and have a more loyal and productive workforce,". Employers who provide options such as telecommuting or flexible work schedules can help employees achieve a better work-life balance.

Consider the best way to achieve balance at work and in your personal life when developing a schedule that works for you. Work-life balance is more about having the flexibility to get things done in your professional life while still having time and energy to enjoy your personal life than it is about dividing the hours in your day evenly between work and personal life. There may be days when you work longer hours so that you can enjoy other activities later in the week.

Here are eight strategies for achieving a better work-life balance, as well as advice on how to be a supportive manager.

1. Recognize that a 'perfect' work-life balance does not exist.

When you hear the phrase "work-life balance," you probably envision having an extremely productive day at work and then leaving early to spend the other half of the day with friends and family. While this may appear to be ideal, it is not always possible.
Strive for a realistic schedule rather than the perfect one. Some days, you may be more focused on work, while others, you may have more time and energy to pursue your hobbies or spend time with your loved ones. Balance is attained over time, not on a daily basis.

"It's critical to stay flexible and constantly assess where you are in relation to your goals and priorities," said Heather Monahan, founder of the #BossinHeels career mentoring group. "Your children may need you at times, and you may need to travel for work at other times, but allowing yourself to be open to redirecting and assessing your needs on any given day is critical in finding balance."

2. Look for a job that you enjoy.

Although work is an expected societal norm, your career should not be limiting. Simply put, if you despise what you do, you will not be happy. You don't have to enjoy every aspect of your job, but it should be interesting enough that you don't dread getting out of bed every morning.

Monahan advised finding a job that you are so passionate about that you would do it for free.

"If your job is draining you and making it difficult to do the things you enjoy outside of work, something is wrong," Monahan said. "You could be working in a toxic environment, for a toxic person, or doing a job you truly dislike.

3. Make your health a top priority.

Your primary concern should be your overall physical, emotional, and mental health. If you suffer from anxiety or depression and believe therapy would benefit you, schedule those sessions, even if it means leaving work early or skipping your evening spin class. If you have a chronic illness, do not be afraid

to call in sick on bad days.
Overworking yourself prevents you
from improving and may force you to
take more days off in the future.
"Putting your health first and foremost
will make you a better employee and
person," Monahan explained. "You will
miss less work and be happier and more
productive when you are there."
Prioritizing your health does not have to
include radical or extreme activities. It
can be as simple as daily meditation or
exercise.

4. Don't be afraid to disconnect.
Cutting ties with the outside world on
occasion allows us to recover from
weekly stress and creates space for new
thoughts and ideas to emerge.

Unplugging can be as simple as practicing transit meditation on your daily commute instead of checking work emails.

When Monahan used to travel with her boss for work, she'd look over to find him reading a novel while she was doing something work-related.

"I didn't realize at the time that he was taking a break and decompressing while I was setting myself up for burnout," Monahan said.

Monahan employs the same strategies now. She emphasized the importance of taking time to relax in order to succeed and will help you feel more energized when you're on the clock.

5. Take a vacation.

Sometimes truly unplugging entails taking a vacation and turning off all work for a while. Whether your vacation is a one-day staycation or a two-week trip to Bali, it's critical to take time off to physically and mentally recharge.

According to the United States. Travel Association's State of American Vacation 2018 study, 52% of employees had unused vacation days at the end of the year. Employees are frequently concerned that taking time off will disrupt the workflow and leave them with a backlog of work when they return. This fear should not prevent you from taking a much-needed break.

"The truth is, there is no nobility in failing to take well-deserved time off from work; the benefits of taking a day off far outweigh the drawbacks," Chancey explained. "With proper planning, you can take time away without worrying about burdening your colleagues or returning to a massive workload."

6. Make time for yourself and your family.

While your job is important, it should not take up all of your time. You were a person before taking this position, and you should prioritize the activities or hobbies that bring you joy. According to Chancey, achieving work-life balance necessitates deliberate action.

"If you don't make time for yourself, you'll never have time to do anything else outside of work," Chancey says. "Regardless of how hectic your schedule is, you ultimately have control over your time and life."

Make a calendar for romantic and family dates when you're planning time with your loved ones. Planning one-on-one time with someone you live with may appear strange, but it will ensure that you spend quality time with them without work-life conflict. Working keeps you busy, but that doesn't mean you should neglect your personal relationships.

"Realize that no one at your company will love or appreciate you in the same way that your loved ones do," Monahan advised. "Also, keep in mind that everyone at work is replaceable, and no matter how important you believe your job is, the company will not miss a beat if you leave tomorrow."

7. Create boundaries and working hours.

To avoid burnout, set boundaries for yourself and your coworkers. Avoid thinking about upcoming projects or responding to company emails as you leave the office. Consider having a separate computer or phone for work, so you can turn it off when you leave. If that isn't possible, keep your work and personal platforms on separate browsers, emails, or filters.

Chancey also suggested that specific work hours be established.

"Whether you work from home or away, it is important to determine when you will work and when you will stop working; otherwise, you may find yourself answering work-related emails late at night, during vacations, or on weekends off," said Chancey.

Chancey recommended informing team members and your manager of any boundaries beyond which you will be unavailable due to personal obligations. This will help ensure that they understand and respect your workplace's boundaries and expectations.

8. Establish goals and priorities (and stick to them).

Set attainable goals by implementing time-management strategies, reviewing your to-do list, and eliminating tasks that are of little to no value.

Pay attention to your most productive times at work and set aside that time for your most important work-related activities. Avoid checking your emails and phone every few minutes, as these are major time-wasters that disrupt your concentration and productivity. Work productivity can be increased by structuring your day, resulting in more free time to relax outside of work.

The rise of the flexible work environment

Those who are successful at balancing their lives frequently point to their flexible work schedules. According to recent research, many employers have given employees more flexibility with their schedules and where they work over the last seven years.

"It is clear that employers continue to struggle with fewer resources for benefits that incur a direct cost," said Ken Matos, lead researcher and senior director of employment research and practice at Families and Work Institute, a nonprofit research organization. "However, they have made it a priority to provide employees with a broader range of benefits that meet their individual and family needs while also improving their health and well-being."

In the long run, employers can benefit from flexibility. "As we look ahead, it is clear that, in order to attract and retain top talent, employers must find ways to offer flexible work options," said Hank Jackson, president and CEO of the Society for Human Resource Management.

"Work-life balance will mean different things to different people," Chancey explained. "Balance is a very personal thing in our always-on world, and only you can decide which lifestyle suits you best."

How to Be a Helpful Boss

We offer four tips to help managers do a better job of supporting their employees' efforts to achieve a healthier work-life balance.

1. Understand what your employees are aiming for. Not everyone strives for the same work-life balance. Discuss each employee's goals with them, and then determine how you can assist them. Some employees may benefit from working remotely a few days per week, whereas others may prefer to change their daily work schedule. It is critical to be open-minded and adaptable.

2. Lead by example. Your employees will follow your example. If you send emails at all hours of the day and night, or work long hours on weekends, your employees will believe the same of them.

3. Inform employees of their options. While employers usually do a good job of emphasizing their work-life balance offerings to prospective employees, the same cannot be said for communicating those initiatives to current employees. Discuss the options available to your employees on a regular basis. Discuss parental leave options with soon-to-be parents as well.

4. Maintain your position at the forefront. It is critical to stay ahead of emerging work-life balance trends. What works today for employees may not work a year from now. Maintain your work-life balance initiatives and provide in-demand benefits. Also, consider providing work-life balance programs.

PART 18

EMPLOYING OTHERS

There will come a time in your entrepreneurial journey when you will require assistance. This is especially true for solo founders and small business owners who want to grow beyond themselves.

Hiring your first employee can alleviate stress and help your small business grow even further. There are plenty of talented professionals available to help you take your venture to the next level, from operations to sales and marketing.

Here's a handy breakdown of the main steps you'll take during the hiring process:

A clear and thorough hiring process is essential for attracting the best new employees. Discover what that procedure entails.
* Your employee hiring procedure should be methodical and well-planned.
* Prepare for the process by researching market hiring conditions and gathering all necessary paperwork.
* When you start the process, consider the specific role you want and how much you are willing to negotiate once

you make an offer. This article is for business owners and hiring managers who want a complete guide to a successful hiring process and are looking to hire new employees.

The hiring process is lengthy and meticulous. If you do it correctly, you will find and hire high-quality candidates who will stay and represent your company as you want. If you don't have experience in human resources, as many small business owners do, you might not know where to start when it comes to hiring. Continue reading for expert advice on employee hiring.

Preparing your company for employee hiring

Whether it's your first or thousandth hire, you should have a defined process in place for recruiting and onboarding. It will become more streamlined as you gain hiring experience and adjust your standard operating procedures accordingly. Take these steps with any new hire to prepare your company for the new employee.

1. Conduct your research.

Rich Deosingh, district president for the Robert Half office in Midtown, New York, suggests researching the local market before looking at open positions within your company.

"Research who is hiring, the economic landscape in your region, and other job postings," Deosingh told Business News Daily. "It will give you an idea of things like salary and market competition - who else is looking for someone with these particular skill sets?"

Once you know that, you can tailor the rest of your hiring process to match what others are doing - or go the other way and stand out so that job candidates are more interested in your company than others.

2. Organize your paperwork.

In some cases, your paperwork may be one-and-done, requiring you to create a template and fill in the necessary information for each new hire. In other cases, the process can be completely automated.

These are some of the forms that may be included in new-hire paperwork.

* **W-4**: This form assists you in determining the appropriate amount of taxes to withhold from each paycheck.

* **I-9:** This document verifies the new hire's employment eligibility.

* **Direct deposit form:** This form provides you with an employee's banking information in order to make payments easier and faster.

* **Non-compete agreement:** A non-compete agreement usually specifies the length of time that an employee is prohibited from working for, consulting for, or engaging in other activities for a

company that does similar business to yours.

* **Employee handbook:** An employee handbook outlines the company's mission, vision, policies, dress code, and code of conduct, among other things.

* **Acknowledgement form:** On this form, the new employee confirms that they have read and understood all of the required documents.

* **Consent to drug testing:** Some employers require new hires to consent to drug testing prior to employment and to agree to random drug testing for the duration of their employment.

Jennifer Walden, director of operations at WikiLawn, said her company has added a home network security checklist, with a field for employees to let the company know if they'll need new hardware to ensure a secure network. "We also make certain that new employees have login information and contact information readily available for anyone they will be working with frequently.

There is a lot of paperwork, but it is all required. The good news is that there are online resources available to help you or your hiring manager with the paperwork.
"Use an HRIS (human resources information system) like Gusto, ADP, or Paycom that provides the HR back-end paperwork to the employee in a self-service mode," said Laura Handrick, Choosing Therapy's HR professional. "There is no reason for a

human to be shuffling paper these days. Online systems with e-signature automate paperwork, ensuring accurate data capture and saving everyone (including the new hire) time."

FYI
The best HR software will include features that will help you streamline employee paperwork and onboarding. You can learn about some of the best options by reading our Gusto review and our Paychex Flex review. Whatever system you use, the key is to have it ready before you begin the hiring process.
"All of these items should be prepared ahead of time and easily accessible online," said Deosingh.

"Communication prior to the first day is critical; if the new hire is required to provide paperwork or identification, this should be noted ahead of time."

Tiger Financial's managing director, Matthew Dailly, agreed with Deosingh. "Using previous hires as a template, review all of the information gathered from them, and then update or add more important documents that have been implemented since," he continued.

3. Outsource if necessary.

It's understandable that not every small business has an HR department or even someone on staff who is familiar with HR procedures. It's preferable to find someone who can do the job well than to make hiring mistakes and end up with high turnover or employees who aren't a good fit.

"For businesses with a one-person HR department, utilizing outsourced resources for recruiting, payroll, benefits administration, and so on can be very helpful to handle the heavy lifting of compliance and reporting requirements for new employees, as well as the company's current employee base," said Karen L. Roberts, SHRM-SCP, director of human resources at Flaster Greenberg PC.

One of the best hiring tips is to leave it to the professionals and work with a reputable HR outsourcing service. "Do not delegate hiring to an inexperienced supervisor," Handrick advised. "Interviewing and recognizing talent is a skill."

Step-by-step procedure for hiring employees

Follow these steps to ensure an efficient hiring process.

1. Determine which positions must be filled.

Sonya Schwartz, founder of Her Norm, believes that this step is critical to avoiding job redundancy within the company.

"The best thing you can do is approach the process with the mindset of filling needs rather than filling desks," Deosingh added. "You want to find the best person for a specific need, not just get someone in and call it a day."

2. Create a recruitment strategy.

You always have options when it comes to recruiting. Dailly suggests first determining whether you will use a recruiting firm. "If not, state 'no agencies, please' on job application forms to save a ton of incoming sales calls."

You may also want to tap into the networks of your current employees. While the hiring process can be time-consuming, you still want to ensure that you find the best candidate for the job. This does not always imply selecting the best candidate overall.

"Recruiters and hiring managers should take their time finding the best candidate for the role rather than settling for the best candidate in the applicant pool," said Lori Rassas, an

HR consultant, executive coach, and author of The Perpetual Paycheck. "If you interview 10 candidates and none are a fit to their role, there will likely be pressure to just pick the best candidate. Hiring managers should defy this pressure and return to the hiring pool to find additional candidates."

3. Create a job description.

Before posting a job, consult with your team managers about the ideal candidate for the job to get a clear picture of what you require. It's also a good idea to notify current employees of the opening. Create a job description that reflects your requirements, including details such as job requirements, responsibilities, and expectations. Include information about your company's core values and culture so that you can find the right cultural fit. According to Dailly, you should also determine the salary so that you can include it in the job description and avoid hiring under- or overqualified candidates.

"In some cases, hiring managers are less than forthcoming about the challenges that the candidate will face, which leads to mistrust, high turnover, and an overall negative impact on workplace culture," Rassas explained. "However, this can be avoided by being clear about what is expected of the person filling the role and ensuring that the candidates you've chosen are capable of fulfilling it."

4. Advertise your job opening.

* Most businesses use career websites to advertise new job openings. Begin by posting the job on your company's website in order to reach a specific audience. If you want to expand your reach, use free and paid online job classifieds. Here are some job posting websites to consider.

* **CareerBuilder**: CareerBuilder, which was founded more than two decades ago, offers resources for both employees and employers, including localized search capacity. The website advertises to over 80 million job seekers worldwide who use its database to search for positions. The posting fee is low and based on the number of positions you are filling for your company.

* **Monster**: Job seekers can search for jobs on Monster by location, skill set, keywords, and job title. To make classifieds stand out, the company has added new features such as video. Pricing varies according to hiring requirements and company size.

* **ZipRecruiter**: You can create a hiring account on ZipRecruiter for free. ZipRecruiter has innovative matching tools to assist you in finding the best candidates for your job posting. All communications are managed by the platform.

* **LinkedIn**: With over 690 million users, LinkedIn has a massive candidate pool. Job postings are free, but you must pay to use the site's more comprehensive recruiting tools.

Tip
Avoid using unregulated websites such as Craigslist because you may receive spam emails and phone calls rather than high-quality applications.

5. Examine applicants.

"When we select and hire our employees, we usually advertise [the job posting] to target specific groups for specific skill sets," Walden explained. "Applications are sent in, and we look through resumes first to immediately rule out anyone who's just completely unqualified or not what we're looking for. If we're undecided, we read cover letters and narrow the field."

If you are unable to find the right candidate for your job opening from the current applicant pool, you may need to revise your job description.

"If you're not seeing the right type of candidate, pivot so you do," Rassas advised. "Yes, work is probably piling up, and yes, you want to get a candidate in the role right away, but a little more effort on the hiring process before extending the offer will save you a lot of time in the long run."

6. The most qualified candidates should be interviewed.

Allow enough time before interviewing candidates to ensure you get the most out of them.

"Inform the applicant about the interview ahead of time so he/she can prepare more," Schwartz advised. "Because you've given them time to prepare, you'll be able to get to know the applicant better and determine if they're a good fit for the role."

Walden stated that the first round of interviews at WikiLawn will take place after they further narrow the applicant pool. Then they conduct a second round of interviews.

"Whether in person or virtual, [the interview] remains the most important part of the hiring process," Deosingh said. "This is the time when you can ask the pertinent questions and, ideally, form a bond with the candidate."

Did You Know?
Some interview questions are illegal.
Brush up on the types of interview
questions you should and should not ask
ahead of time.

7. Follow up with the interviewees.
This stage isn't just for calling or
emailing the applicants. According to
Deosingh, post-interview evaluation is
also critical.
"Don't get caught up in the halo effect
and be blinded by any potential flaws,"
he advised. "Maintain perspective and
take everything into account - not just
the interview or resume but the totality
of what you've seen. Get feedback from
others, but keep it to a small group to
avoid brain drain."

Follow-up can take many forms. It could be as simple as a thank-you note for the interviewee's time, all the way up to a formal job offer

8. Increase the duration of the job offer.

You want to move quickly if you've interviewed a large number of people and found high-quality candidates for the position.

"Make a decision right away," Deosingh advised. "Make certain that all stakeholders (if applicable) are available to interview and provide feedback in a timely manner. The demand for skilled employees remains high, and if you wait too long, you may lose a potential hire to other opportunities."

It is also important to be specific with your offer.

"Make sure to make an irresistible job offer," Schwartz advised. "The majority of high-quality employees demand higher pay and good benefits."

FYI

Offering a competitive employee benefits package not only helps you attract top talent, but it can also help you retain current employees.

Prepare to negotiate salary and employee benefits, regardless of how good you believe the offer is.

"Give the potential employee time to consider your offer, and if he/she does not agree, try to negotiate," Schwartz advised. "Every negotiation should be a win-win situation."

9. Perform a background check. Before bringing the person into your workplace, you should conduct a background check to ensure there are no significant red flags.

"You can conduct a background check if you believe the prospective applicant is qualified for the position," Schwartz said. "This will validate your decision."

Hiring remote employees

Hiring remote workers has become more common for businesses in the aftermath of the COVID-19 pandemic, but it comes with its own set of challenges. You'll need to make a few changes when guiding remote candidates through the hiring process. "While the core principles of onboarding remain the same," Deosingh explained. "They are unable to see your physical space. The opportunity to see the space and get acclimated to the physical location is an important part of the onboarding process."

Here are some ways to make the process more engaging for remote hires:

1. Prepare the employee for their first day. When it comes to technology, make sure their employee credentials and logins are up to date and that they have all of the necessary equipment they need before day one.

2. Greet them warmly. This may appear basic, but it can go a long way. Set up a video introduction with the new hire's team to make them feel welcome. Remember that they are entering your organization at a completely different point than previous employees. Make them feel welcome even if you can't be in the same physical location.

3. Be available. It's easy to say you're available while failing to demonstrate it in practice. Your new hire will undoubtedly have questions. If they can't walk into your office or lean over to ask their teammates, they must feel comfortable reaching out via remote communication channels. Over

Communicating information and making yourself available and open to questions is critical when onboarding new hires remotely.

Because the new employee will not have handouts or physical paperwork with them, it is critical to provide a thorough and clear online guide.

Recruiting your new employee
These are the five most important aspects of onboarding:
1. Provide an orientation. Although it may be distant, a general overview of the company is essential for any new hire to hear.
2. Describe your company's core values and expectations. This is always important when embarking on a journey

with a new hire. The sooner you establish expectations, the better off your company and your new employee will be.

3. Go over job responsibilities. You probably covered a lot of this during the interview process, but it is useful to go into more detail about employee expectations now that they have the job.

4. Assign them a starting project. Many new employees are eager to get started. Instead of having them sit through orientations and company overviews at the start, give them something to get their teeth into right away.

5. Assign a mentor. Find a mentor in a position similar to the new employee's to provide them with someone who can answer their questions and point them in the right direction.

According to Roberts, her company's onboarding process begins with a welcome package (an offer letter, new-hire paperwork, benefits information, and an employee handbook) and continues through orientation and training to the employee's first day on the job.

"It should include introductions to key staff members, employer resources, office tours, and anything else that will help a new hire assimilate to their new role as a member of your team," she explained.

According to Schwartz, onboarding should also include any necessary personal data encoding, an explanation of your company's mission and vision, training on standard operating procedures, and, if applicable, the distribution of supplies and uniforms.

"Onboarding is about making a good first impression and engaging the new hire in their commitment to work with your company," Handrick said. "It's more than just paperwork." She went on to say that you should create a checklist of every task and activity that will make the new hire feel welcome, productive, and want to stay.

Handrick also stated that, while first-week activities tend to focus on paperwork, the true value of onboarding

is what happens in the first 30-90 days
and its long-term effects.

PART 19

SERIAL ENTREPRENEURSHIP

A serial entrepreneur is someone who
starts numerous new businesses in a
short period of time. A businessperson
is someone who constantly pursues new

ideas and works on them at the same time.

What Does Serial Entrepreneur Mean?

Traditional entrepreneurs are individuals who conceive, plan, organize, and execute a given idea and work on it on a daily basis either until the business is properly consolidated or until they leave as senior managers. A serial entrepreneur, on the other hand, is someone who pursues a business idea but does not devote himself entirely to it for an extended period of time; instead, he delegated most of the day-to-day operations to others and devotes his time to the next idea. They typically have many ongoing projects at various stages of development, and their goal is to empower someone else to take over and develop the idea.

Serial entrepreneurship has been studied as a business phenomenon, and it is a popular trend. Serial entrepreneurs include well-known business figures such as Steve Jobs and Elon Musk. However, there are risks to being a serial entrepreneur if your leadership skills are insufficient to empower others to do the day-to-day work properly, or if there is no checks and balances system in place. Also, people who are easily distracted or undisciplined may lose focus, and all businesses may suffer as a result of a lack of attention during the development stages of each.

Example

Phil is a marketing expert with over 15 years of experience in the advertising industry. His in-depth understanding of how the industry works has inspired him to launch new ventures. Phil considers himself an entrepreneur, having founded three businesses.

The first is a digital marketing firm that specializes in social media management and content creation.
The second is a BTL marketing agency specializing in creative advertising, and the third is a marketing consulting firm.

Phil is a serial entrepreneur, so these will not be his only businesses, but in order to grow them, he hired three experienced individuals to manage and grow each of them.

What exactly is a serial entrepreneur?

It's not uncommon for people to start businesses, fail, and then try again. A serial entrepreneur, on the other hand, is generally regarded as a different breed because they frequently have a track record of launching multiple successful businesses.

Serial entrepreneurs start several businesses one after the other, as opposed to starting one venture and focusing on it for many years, as a typical entrepreneur would. They may also sell their businesses once they have reached a certain level of maturity. They may retain ownership while delegating day-to-day managerial responsibilities to others. If the business is underperforming, they may close it and move on to the next idea.

There is no set number of businesses that someone must start to be considered a serial entrepreneur, but three may be a good starting point. Moreover, not all businesses must succeed or generate profits. Most serial entrepreneurs, however, have at least a couple of significant and long-lasting successes to their name.

The Advantages and Drawbacks of Being a Serial Entrepreneur

While each startup is unique, there are some steps that are common to most, if not all, entrepreneurial ventures. Serial entrepreneurs learn the hard way, sometimes by making mistakes, how to get a business idea in motion and off the ground.

Along with skills development, they make contacts with investors, talented employees, and others who can assist them with their next venture.

Because of the value that experienced startup leaders bring, venture capital investors prefer to back companies founded by serial entrepreneurs. This preference is not limited to serial entrepreneurs whose previous startups have all been successful. According to this viewpoint, failure can be a good teacher, and past failure can pave the way for future success.

Serial entrepreneurship can have both limitations and risks, as well as benefits. For one thing, a serial entrepreneur who builds and sells a startup that later becomes extremely successful may miss out on the opportunity to amass enormous wealth by cashing out too soon.

Another risk is that a serial entrepreneur will be distracted by an idea for a new startup soon after starting one. As a result, the entrepreneur may fail to pay enough attention to the first business, causing it to flounder and fail.

Examples of Serial Entrepreneurs

Many well-known entrepreneurs have gained prominence as a result of their long-term involvement with a single startup. Bill Gates, co-founder of Microsoft, is an example of a serial entrepreneur. Serial entrepreneurs, on the other hand, have a unique way of attracting public attention due to their repeated, sometimes spectacular, success in a variety of fields.

Richard Branson is a well-known serial entrepreneur who has launched hundreds of businesses ranging from airlines to soft drinks, all under the Virgin label of his first company, a mail-order record company. Many of Branson's new ventures have failed to gain traction. However, few other serial entrepreneurs can match Branson's multiple wins in such diverse fields.

Oprah Winfrey is another serial entrepreneur who leveraged an early success to build a diverse empire, this time in media. Winfrey has established herself as a major player in television production, cable television, and magazine publishing.

Elon Musk, a more recent arrival on the scene, began as a web software entrepreneur, moved to online financial services, and has since disrupted industries ranging from tunnel construction to space transportation. He did, however, join Tesla, the electric car company that may be his most notable venture, soon after it was founded.

Bottom Line

Serial entrepreneurs move from one new business idea to the next, starting companies and then selling, closing them, or delegating management to others. While their track record may not be one of perfect repeat success, serial entrepreneurs' hard-won experience and demonstrated diligence make them appealing to some new venture investors.

A serial entrepreneur is someone who is exceptionally creative in coming up with new business ideas and working hard to develop those ideas into a new venture.
This is someone who can fail repeatedly. This is someone who can

learn from their mistakes and turn them into greatness.

Everyone cannot create something amazing with new ideas, and not everyone can run multiple businesses at the same time.

Only a'serial entrepreneur' with a passion for innovation and great ideas will be able to make the magic happen.

How Do Serial Entrepreneurs Run Several Businesses?

Just because a serial entrepreneur came up with a business idea doesn't mean they'll be the ones carrying it out on a daily basis.

Once the business venture begins to gain traction, the serial entrepreneur will hire employees to run this specific company. This way, they will be able to devote sufficient time and attention to each of their business ventures.

We know what you're thinking. Why would a successful businessperson consider starting something new from scratch, especially when they are doing so well with their current project?

That is what qualifies them as a serial entrepreneur. They want to test all of their new ideas and turn them into something hugely successful.

This allows them not only to test whether their new idea will work in the market, but also to give them more exposure and see how much better they can get at multitasking.

And, of course, who doesn't want to make some extra money?

And being a serial entrepreneur does not imply that you are only starting new businesses on your own.

This could also imply working together on a business idea. It could also imply that you are launching multiple products in the market under the same company name.

A serial entrepreneur is someone who enjoys innovation and managing multiple business ideas at once (whether these are new products, new services, or a new subpart of your already existing company).

What Is the Difference Between a Traditional and a Serial Entrepreneur?

The first and most significant distinction between the two types of entrepreneurs is their passion.

A traditional entrepreneur does not have the same drive as a serial entrepreneur to launch multiple business ventures at once.

Here are a few characteristics that distinguish a serial entrepreneur from a traditional entrepreneur:

They Are Enthusiastic

Serial entrepreneurs are passionate about their business ideas and will go to great lengths to see them succeed.

For example, when they have a new venture idea, they begin working on the business strategies to make it a reality. They use their resources, including their capital, to launch the new business. They are ecstatic about their new business idea, which motivates them to work tirelessly in the same direction. When their new venture begins to show signs of progress, they tend to move on to another idea while leaving the current venture in the hands of a team.

They Are Not Only Driven By Money
A serial entrepreneur is motivated by more than just monetary goals.
This is not to say that they do not want to make a profit, but they are not solely concerned with monetary gain.

Because they have so many ideas and have strategized their business plans, the only thing on their mind is how to make their business idea a successful hit.

That is what motivates them. They want to make their startup a success story. After that, they move on to their next business idea.

They Are Super Connectors

Serial entrepreneurs excel at networking and connecting with others, as well as connecting others.

They believe that as good networkers, we have two ears and one mouth and that we should use them both proportionally. They listen to people's needs and concerns and look for ways to assist them.

To truly build an empire, you must be able to form genuine relationships with powerful people and provide value to each of them.

They Fail, But Try Again

It's important to experiment with new business concepts. A traditional entrepreneur may be hesitant to invest money and time in a new business idea because they are concerned about its failure.

A serial entrepreneur, on the other hand, is daring and takes on the challenge of launching a new venture and testing it in the business market.

They are confident in their idea and their ability to make their various ventures successful. As a result, they can better analyze market conditions and make business decisions as a result.

They Are Good Team Players
Being a serial entrepreneur does not require you to be the sole leader of a business idea.

It is beneficial to be a team player and accept assistance from people or partners who can help you achieve your goal of turning your new business idea into a successful venture.

For example, if you have an idea related to an industry about which you don't have enough knowledge or expertise to practically demonstrate it, the best way to proceed would be to collaborate with someone who knows that industry inside and out.

You will not only benefit from their expertise in that field, but you will also learn a lot from them, which will help you in the future of your business.

They Utilize Every Resource Efficiently

Many small business owners want to be the only ones running their own operation.

They are unwilling to involve others because they would have to pay them. Serial entrepreneurs, on the other hand, take the risk and use all of the resources at their disposal.

There are numerous freelancers available in the market who are eager to work on major projects for your company. You can hire them for a very low fee, and they can actually assist you in making your work much easier. And this is precisely what a serial entrepreneur makes full use of.

For example, they may hire a freelance social media manager to manage their Facebook or Instagram handles, ensuring that your social media presence is active and up to date.

They Are Innovators

A new business idea does not always turn out to be a one-of-a-kind one. However, you can make innovations and turn something ordinary into something extraordinary. That is precisely what serial entrepreneurs do when they have an idea and discover that it already exists in the market. Serial entrepreneurs attempt to innovate in order to make their idea more unique or to help build something that does not yet exist. That is why they are referred to as innovators.

They Are Strategists
Running multiple businesses at the same time necessitates the development of strategies to manage them all. You cannot expect a new business to run on its own.
You need a strategy, a business plan to help your new venture grow.

Serial entrepreneurs, of course, understand the importance of strategizing their business ideas by hiring the appropriate staff to help them cope with their various business ventures after gaining experience.

If They Can do it, You Can Too

Some entrepreneurs believe that they will not be able to achieve the success that they desire. However, if you look around at all the success stories, you will be motivated to be like them, if not better than them.

Oprah Winfrey is one of the living legends of Serial Entrepreneurship. She worked as a television anchor before establishing 'Harpo Productions, Inc.

She is well-known for her talk show, 'The Oprah Winfrey Show,' and has served as an inspiration to many serial entrepreneurs. She is not only the co-founder of the well-known cable channel 'Oxygen,' but she also launched her 'OWN' Oprah Winfrey Network in 2011.

Wrap Up

Starting a successful business is not easy for anyone. It takes a lot of hard work and teamwork to get it to its full potential.

If you have a new business idea and want to test it out, you must be confident in your ability to make it a reality. You can't start something if you're not sure about it.

So be confident in your business concept and in yourself. You've got this!

Check out The Entrepreneur Cooperative if you want to have more conversations like this. It's our group of inspiring entrepreneurs assisting other amazing entrepreneurs in connecting and overcoming the challenges that life throws at us.

Acknowledgement

First and foremost, I would like to express my heartfelt gratitude to Almighty God for allowing us to successfully complete this Business Plan. Then I'd like to thank Dr. John Gray, our honorable supervisor and lecturer at the College of Tourism and Hotel Management, who has always encouraged us to create an appropriate Business Plan, as well as those friends who have provided me with vital information to create this Business Plan.

We would like to thank our creator for allowing us to finish our work, particularly for assisting us during difficult times.

After overcoming all obstacles and adversity, we have finally arrived at our destination. We are pleased to announce that we have completed our business plan report. Without a doubt, we would like to state that ample knowledge and experiences were obtained during the completion of this course. Though it is undeniably difficult for us to complete the task, it is worthwhile and we learn a lot. We are grateful to the Almighty God for His divine guidance, which has enabled us to complete our business plan.

We would like to thank Miss Kylie Greener, our entrepreneurship walkabout, for her guidance, support, and advice. She also shares her knowledge and experience to ensure that we complete this business plan on time in accordance to the requirements for the completion of HPD 228.

Recalling our experiences while working on this report, we were able to create a strong bond of friendship among our team members. The strong bond that has been formed and the cooperation that exists greatly assist us in achieving our goals. All of our teammates play critical roles in our success.

We'd also like to thank our family, especially our parents, for their patience and encouragement, as well as our grandparents for praying for us through thick and thin.

We dedicate this work to everyone who is always eager to learn, has the courage to keep studying, and believes in God and Allah at all times.

www.ingramcontent.com/pod-product-compliance
Lightning Source LLC
Chambersburg PA
CBHW071131220526
45467CB00015B/830